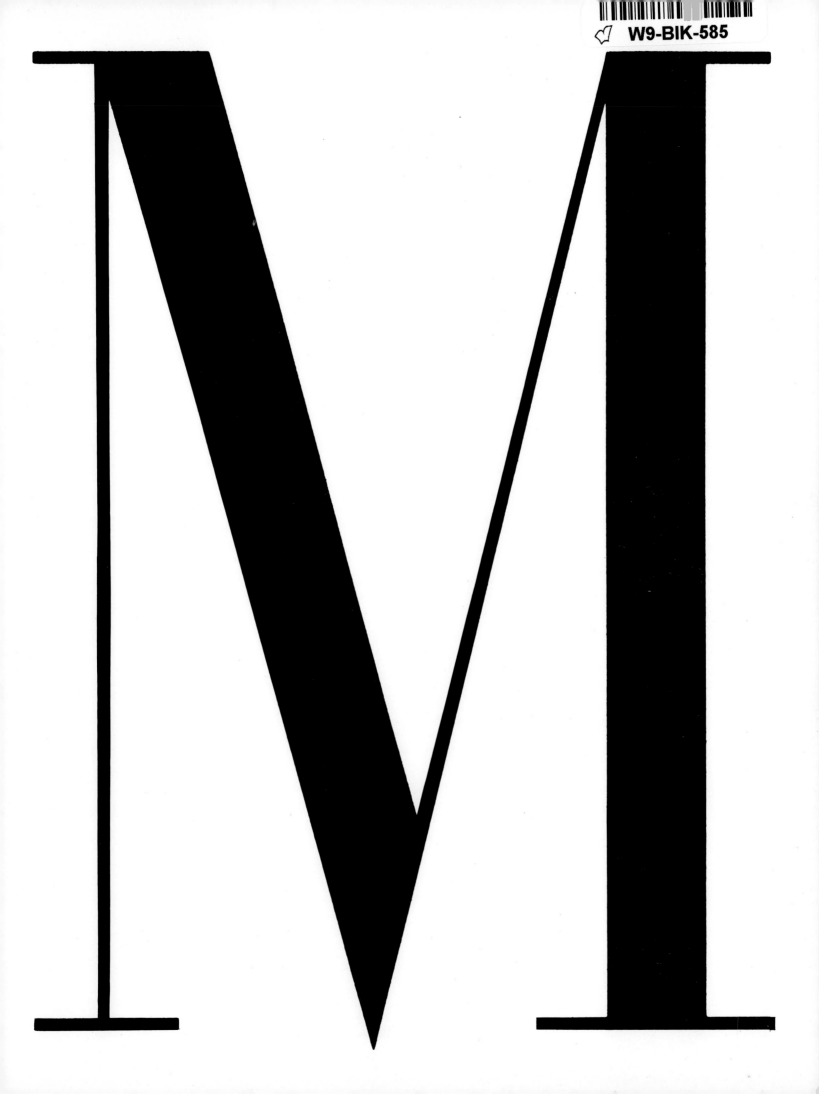

Exclusive Distributors
Book Sales Limited,
8/9 Frith Street,
London W1V 5TZ, UK.
Music Sales Corporation,
257 Park Avenue South,
New York, NY 10010, USA.
The Five Mile Press,
22 Summit Road,
Noble Park,
Victoria 3174, Australia.
To the Music Trade only:
Music Sales Limited,
8/9 Frith Street,
London W1V 5TZ, UK.

Visit Omnibus Press at
www.omnibuspress.com.uk

Printed and bound in
Singapore

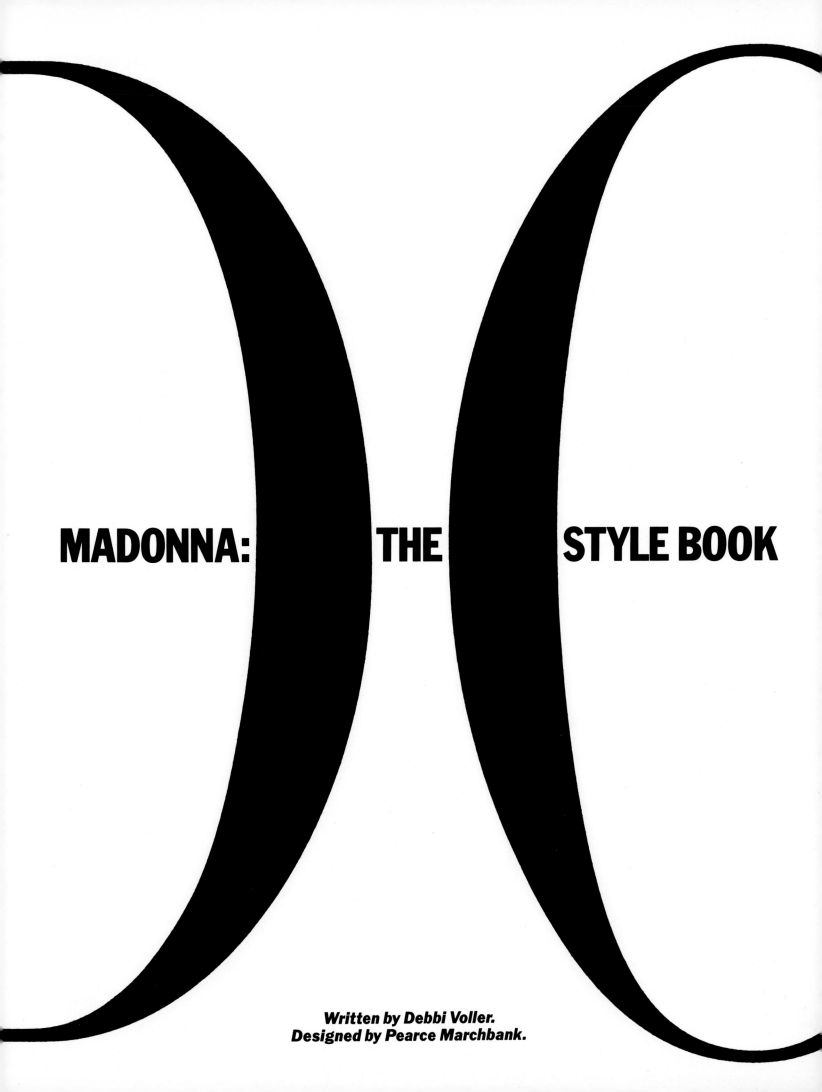

MADONNA: THE STYLE BOOK

Written by Debbi Voller.
Designed by Pearce Marchbank.

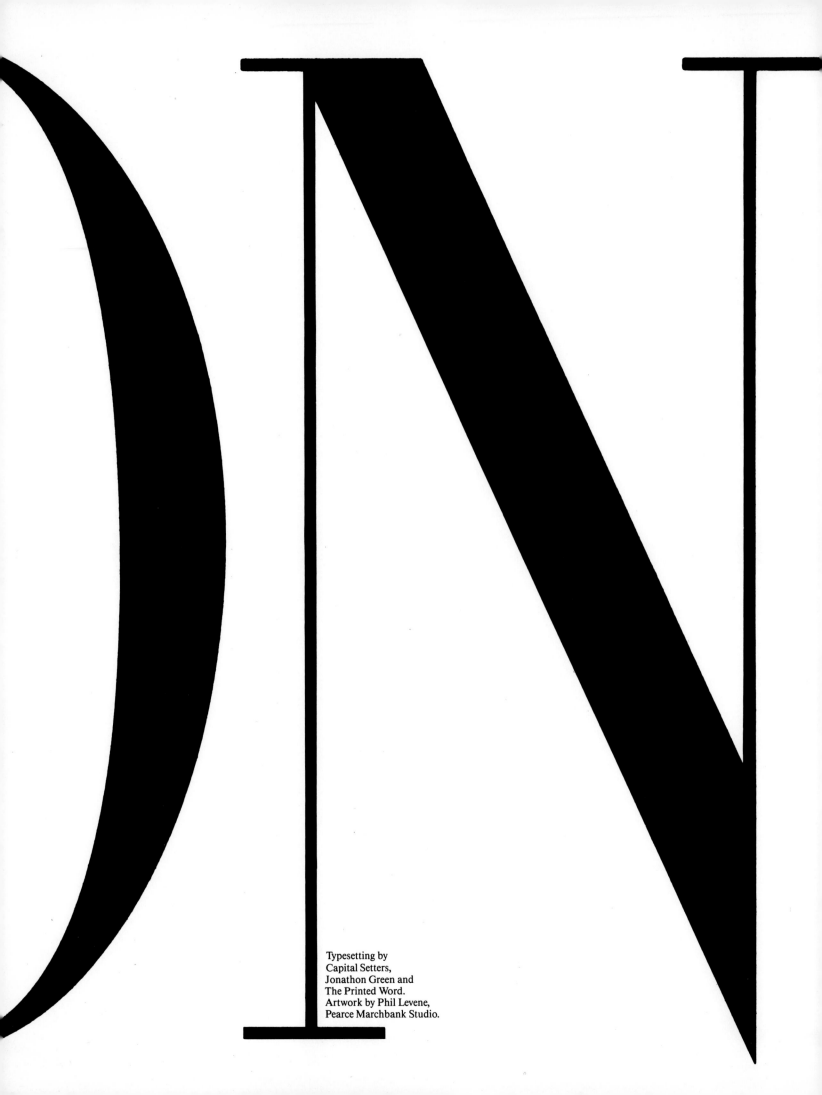

Typesetting by
Capital Setters,
Jonathon Green and
The Printed Word.
Artwork by Phil Levene,
Pearce Marchbank Studio.

Edited by Chris Charlesworth.
Picture research by David Brolan.
Photographs supplied by
All-Action Pictures,
Associated Press,
The Kobal Collection,
London Features International,
Barry Plummer, Pictorial Press,
Rex Features, Starfile and
Pearce Marchbank Studio.
Fashion sketches by
Robert Eldridge.

**Madonna Louise
Veronica Ciccone
in 1978.**

**Madonna as a
seven-year-old
bridesmaid.**

"I have never met anyone with such spark, such charisma. Madonna is superb and surprising, always impeccable... even fashion models don't possess this constant perfection."
Jean Paul Gaultier, 1990.

"If she couldn't sing she would be a great stripper. She makes me want to go out on the streets tomorrow and wear my underpants over my trousers."
Ruby Wax, comedienne.

Since her reign as role model extraordinaire was launched in 1983 with tongue-in-cheek tart outfits made from fishnet and lace, Catholic accessories, bras and trade-mark belly-button, Madonna has provoked a mixed bag of highly-charged emotions. Once hailed as a 'Dynamic Diva', and crowned both 'Myth America' and 'The Queen of Sleaze', her shrewd and ceaseless determination to succeed, coupled with her ever-evolving and ever-ambiguous image, has made sure that – whether you like her or not – Madonna is omnipresent. Not since Marilyn Monroe has anyone managed to so saturate the media and our culture.

Madonna's record company, Warner Brothers, declared her an icon for the eighties and a goddess for the nineties. "Give or take the Queen, Princess Diana and Elizabeth Taylor, Madonna is, for better or worse, the most famous woman on earth," confirmed the *Daily Mail* in May 1991 when Madonna shone as the brightest star at the annual Cannes Film Festival. Blatantly flirting with the images of her favoured film stars, she was described as a mini-Marilyn', and a 'baby Dietrich'. But perhaps the most accurate description for a woman so completely in control of her life was that she was 'a cross between Mae West and Margaret Thatcher'.

Madonna was never a conventional beauty. With her self-critical and characteristic iron will, she honed her once cherubic body into Olympian perfection, but at five foot four and a half, she was too short to have ever considered a career as a professional model. Within that diminutive stature, however, lies an Amazon warrior spirit that inspired legions of 'wannabes'. "Had she been more beautiful, or more talented, she would probably be forgotten by now," wrote journalist Julie Burchill in an issue of the *Mail*. "But it was her perceived lack of these things that made her realise that only hard work would get her where she wanted to be... and keep them guessing."

Like Marilyn Monroe and Brigitte Bardot, whose novel treatment of *men* as playthings liberated women in the fifties, Madonna luxuriated in her sexuality. Although she never set out to be a role model, she inadvertently kindled a new kind of feminism for the eighties, as thousands of teenage girls began to look up to her and mirror her image. Madonna's erotic pull sparked something in the female spirit. It was as if a dramatic new awakening had taken place. By looking soft and sexy but acting tough and smart, she encouraged women to compete in a man's world with their femininity intact; to fight for a true equality by being true to themselves. As her career developed, Madonna's fans weren't so much obsessed with her clothes as with the statement that the clothes were making. They

wanted to mirror her ambition and strength of character, for Madonna was living proof that you could transcend your limitations and imperfections by believing in yourself. Madonna's fellow forty-somethings now look sexy to please themselves – and the joke is on the men. For Madonna helped defuse "typical" male fantasies by taking them to extremes with coned bullet bras, see-through tops and, in her controversial *Sex* book, casual nudity in public places.

One wonders how fashion in the nineties would have evolved if Madonna had never come along. Perhaps the phenomenon of underwear-as-outerwear would still have emerged but, without Madonna as its role model, it would surely have remained the self-indulgent whim of some outlandish designer, rather than becoming a mainstream style for body-conscious consumers. Without Madonna the female wardrobe would still be open to extreme sexist interpretation; old attitudes die hard, but she helped to speed their departure.

Religion continues to play a leading role in Madonna's style. Sexuality and spirituality are inseparable in her mind and she united them by wearing a crucifix with a corset, a rosary with a bra. This self-confessed fallen Catholic, who had her first crush on Jesus Christ and thought nuns were sexy superhumans, has become an icon herself. Fighting for freedom of expression, she is a wonderfully subversive presence as she declares, "If you're afraid of me, then you're afraid of what I make you feel." Beyond her controversial love-to-shock appeal, there is wink and positive message behind everything Madonna does.

"She's the Billy Liar who made it, the glorious product of her own grandiose imagination. That heady mixture of narcissism and exhibitionism draws people. She loves herself and wants everybody to love her too. We are invited to an orgy of adulation."
Nigella Lawson, Evening Standard, July 1991.

On a more superficial level, Madonna became unbeatable in the self-promotion stakes; the ultimate focus puller. Driven by an intense fear of being mediocre, Madonna built herself into a myth and then declared that enough was enough. She attempted to demystify show business and became more human in the eyes of the world by making the film *In Bed With Madonna*. Behind-the-scenes concert footage stripped away the make-up and the razzle-dazzle to reveal a vulnerable, material and lonely Madonna, as well as a brazen, bossy and precocious star.

Now the mother of a baby daughter, the demystification process continues at a steady pace. Time seems to have eroded Madonna's harsher edges and the inward looking Madonna of the late nineties seems more mature, more graceful, more gentle, more honest, more human. Her profile may be slightly lower but we still listen when she speaks, and with the ill-conceived *Sex* book episode behind her and her acclaimed performance in *Evita* a glistening jewel in her crown, she is still a heroine of colossal proportions.

THE LOOK

The periodical recreation of the Madonna image is now an eagerly awaited event, and each new look is worshipped and adored by fans and fashion houses alike. The Madonna persona has evolved from rags to untold riches, and though she no longer has to improvise with second-hand clothes from thrift shops, Madonna still has an uncanny ability to spot a promising underground trend and mould it into something that is uniquely her own. By the time everyone else has caught on, she leaves the mainstream behind by reinventing herself yet again.

Whether she is pouring herself into tight Monroe dresses, or writhing splay-legged in fishnets and a Gaultier bodysuit, Madonna has become the world's most prominent fashion force and dominant female sex symbol. And yet when her first record 'Everybody' was released back in 1982, nobody could fit a face or an image to her name – because her record company didn't want the public to know what she looked like.

Madonna's appearance was a secret because she sounded black, and 'Everybody' achieved its initial success through radio play on black stations. It was a similar situation to that which faced Elvis Presley when *his* first record, 'That's All Right', was released in 1954. Consequently there was no video and no picture on Madonna's record sleeve. But Madonna was happy enough – soul was one of her first influences – and not just the sound of soul.

"When I was a little girl I wished I was black. I was living in Pontiac, Michigan and all of my friends were black, and all the music I listened to

"Why do I keep reinventing myself? I don't think it's a question of getting tired of myself... I'm just acting out different parts of my personality."

Facing page: Madonna's grand entrance at the 1991 Cannes Film Festival left no one in any doubt who was *the* star of the event.

was black. I was incredibly jealous of all my black girlfriends because they could have braids in their hair that stuck up everywhere. So I would go through this incredible ordeal of putting wire in my hair and braiding it so that I could make my hair stick up."

Madonna's early yearnings for an offbeat style found a white role model in Nancy Sinatra, who had a hit in 1966 with 'These Boots Were Made For Walkin'. Madonna longed to look like a child of the sixties and wear "go-go boots, mini-skirts, blonde hair and fake eyelashes." But her stepmother would only allow her to wear plain dresses that matched her sisters' and Madonna felt like "the quintessential Cinderella".

Seeking escapism in the old Hollywood movies that were shown at local revival houses, Madonna fell under the spell of the strong and beautiful sirens of the silver screen: Greta Garbo, Marlene Dietrich, Grace Kelly and Marilyn Monroe, all paragons of femininity back in the Thirties, Forties and Fifties. But for the moment Madonna's self-image was far from glamorous. She certainly didn't see herself as a potential icon. "I didn't really like myself that much. I didn't think I was beautiful... I wasn't born with a perfect body... I always wanted to be taller and I felt like a shrimp."

Madonna also admired Ann-Margret and Brigitte Bardot. "I wanted to make my hair blonde, wear tight sweaters and pointed bras." Forbidden by her stepmother to wear make-up and nylon stockings, Madonna tried on fancy clothes when she visited wealthier friends. She turned her school uniform into an instrument of rebellion by hitching up her skirt to reveal colourful, sexy underwear, and in the school cloakroom she changed into stockings and applied make up.

In her early adolescence, Madonna cut off her shoulder-length brown hair, pierced her ears, and wore oddly coloured knee socks. She finally burst out of the fashion closet at a school talent show when she shocked her father by dancing in a bikini with fluorescent flowers painted all over her body.

Attending ballet classes in Rochester when she was 14, Madonna met a teacher who was to become the first great direct influence on her life: the late Christopher Flynn. He recognised that there was something special about Madonna, even though... "she was very young... barely out of adolescence, a plain little child with short, kind of dishwater blonde hair. She looked like the most innocent child in the world."

Flynn was a Catholic homosexual. He introduced Madonna to the sublime world of the arts and the seedy gay clubs in downtown Detroit. "He gave me a sense of culture and style... he was the first person that told me I was beautiful, that told me I was special, and that made me look at myself in a different way. I was feeling horribly unattractive and uninteresting and 'unfabulous' and he said 'God you're beautiful!'"

Left: Nancy Sinatra, an early role model for the young Madonna.

Facing page: Early use of the Boy Toy tag, Madonna's droll comment on the battle of the sexes, to promote her first album.

Feeling a little more adventurous, Madonna dared to dress up as a "floozy", a term used by her disapproving stepmother who accused her of looking cheap and vulgar every time she wore just "a little lip gloss or opaque pantihose". Madonna and her girlfriend of the time "got dressed to the nines. We got bras and stuffed them, so our breasts were over-large and wore really tight sweaters – we were ten-cent, sweater-girl floozies. We wore tons of lipstick and really badly applied make up and huge beauty marks and did our hair up like Tammy Wynette."

Madonna spent one summer with her younger uncles in Bay City, where she was given the freedom to experiment even further. "I was watching my uncles' rock'n'roll band wearing tight jeans for the first time in my life. I smoked a cigarette, not too successfully, I started plucking my eyebrows and I started feeling like, 'Yeah, this is it, I'm cool'."

When she was 17 and studying dance at the performing arts school in Michigan, Madonna refused to conform to the traditional image of a pretty ballerina in pink tights with neatly bunned hair. "I cut my hair really short and I'd grease it so it would be sticking up, and I'd rip my tights so there were runs all over them, and I'd make a big cut down the middle of my leotard and put teeny little safety-pins all the way up it. Anything to stand out and say, 'I'm not like you, OK?'"

During those well-documented days in New York when Madonna struggled to make her mark – first as a dancer and then as a singer – she continued to make statements with her clothes. Shopping in cheap and trashy thrift shops she bought ripped up shirts, oversized men's clothes, khaki pants, high-heeled shoes, and rags for her hair which was ratted and dark. She was influenced by punk but moving it in her own direction.

"I used to be just a brazen, outgoing, crazy lass, and I went out of my way to get attention... I loved getting dressed up and going out on the street and walking around and seeing the visual effect I had on people."

One of her old boyfriends, Dan Gilroy, remembers the outfit she was wearing when he met her at a party in 1979. "A kind of circus outfit, very short with a blue tutu, and dark blue leggings... and she had olive oil in her hair which made it quite strange and matted."

In the late seventies, a new urban subculture started to explode in New York and Madonna was quick to enter into its spirit. Latin and black kids from the Lower East Side and the Bronx were break-dancing to hip hop music on every street corner, and spraying their names on every available surface, from brick walls to subway trains.

Madonna hung out in Latin clubs and mixed with graffiti artists. "I got in the habit of carrying markers and writing my name everywhere, and everybody had their name on a belt buckle." Nicknames were chosen to create a public ident-

Above: When Madonna first arrived in New York she shopped in thrift stores but still managed to create startling and original outfits. Here her hair is matted and flattened with olive oil, a punkish idea that would not have been out of place on the Kings Road, London.

Facing page: From the very beginning Madonna exposed a variety of different bras to public view. Here's one of most erotic: black, see-through and very sexy.

Madonna seemed to have a weight problem when she first emerged in the New York discos. Here promoting her first album, with 'Toy Boy' belt and dramatic heart-covered veil.

Until the arrival of the Keith Haring inspired outfits that were a highlight of the 'Like A Virgin' tour, Madonna went through a period of experimentation. Her arms festooned with dozens of bracelets, Madonna layered different T-shirts and tops, and almost always wore leggings beneath short skirts or dresses.

ity for the street, and this was when Madonna chose the famous BOY TOY tag for her belt buckle, which was to cause so much controversy. She wore Adidas sneakers with different coloured laces, nylon tracksuits in bright colours, fishnet midriff tops that exposed her belly button, studded belts and bracelets, leather caps, and gloves with the fingers cut off. "Eventually when I started becoming an image in pictures, it was a combination of the dance and the ragamuffin and the New Wave and Puerto Rican street style."

Says Michael Rosenblatt, former talent scout for Sire Records who instigated her record deal, "I had been told about this wild-looking girl who had her own look and was very beautiful... whatever that certain something is, she had it. She had more of it than I'd ever seen."

Madonna was a name without a face when she had her first hit with 'Holiday' at the end of 1983. She said at the time, "In America, my record company don't know how to push me, whether to push me as a disco artist or as New Wave because of the way I look."

England had no such trouble coming to terms with Madonna's image when she made her first appearance on *Top Of The Pops*, because it was totally in tune with the London club scene. Raggedy 'hard times' street fashions, ripped up clothes, ratted hair and dreadlocks had been around for some time, championed by trend spotters like Malcolm McLaren, and worn by groups like Culture Club and Bow Wow Wow. Young girls throughout the UK had been busy braiding their hair in imitation of the asexual Boy George – but there was clearly room for a new and female role model.

Right on cue Madonna appeared with a raunchy dance routine, gyrating in a black fishnet skirt, midriff top and thick fall-down socks, dripping with jewellery, and shamelessly flashing her bra and belly button. Her streaked blonde hair was unkempt and wild, tied here and there with a mess of rags, and her thick eyebrows were unplucked and untamed. In subsequent videos and pop pin-ups Madonna flaunted a selection of crucifix earrings – several in each lobe – and Catholic rosaries worn casually as necklaces. Her forearms were strewn with dozens of rubber and studded bracelets, and slung low around her waist she wore studded belts and the BOY TOY buckle. Lacy tights hadn't been in fashion since the sixties, but now Madonna revived the look with lacy leggings worn under ripped-up jeans and clinging, cotton hipster skirts. Colourful lace bras were worn under matching midriff tops in day-Glo colours, worn off the shoulder to expose the bra straps. It was an original but easy look to follow, and it soon caught on.

Pop magazines questioned Madonna at length about her style. What kind of clothes did she like? "I like athletic sports wear, I've gone through that with all my Puerto Rican boyfriends. I read all the fashion magazines and I follow designers like

Vivienne Westwood and Jean-Paul Gaultier. I don't have much time to go shopping though, and half the stuff I want, I can't get in New York."

Did she design her own look and hair? "Oh yeah. Do you think someone else could come up with this?" Was the image calculated? "I didn't want to be seen as a dumb blonde or as a totally aggressive woman. It's a balance of masculine and feminine qualities... I wouldn't call it calculated. My image is a natural extension of my performance." And finally, how did she feel about being a sex symbol? "I feel slightly entertained... it's funny!"

With the release of the controversial 'Like A Virgin' single and album towards the end of 1984, Madonna teasingly revamped the traditional white wedding dress by posing as a far-from-blushing bride in a series of photographs by Steven Meisel. Glancing coyly at the camera for her album cover, she wore a white push-up, half-cup bustier made from fishnet and lace, with a full skirt, long lacy fingerless gloves and BOY TOY buckle.

Outraged moralists had the first of what would soon become a deluge of Madonna-induced fits of pique and accused her of being a shameless sex kitten, but throughout her career, Madonna has always loved to play cat and mouse with conventional stereotypes. The *Like A Virgin* album cover was a classic example. Who was Madonna pretending to be – the virgin or the whore? These were the two extreme images of woman she had grown up with as a Catholic girl.

"In the beginning I was being provocative, being a clown. I like to combine things in a humorous way... I like irony. I like the way things can be taken on different levels... 'Like A Virgin' was always absolutely ambiguous."

Madonna's quirky sense of humour went way above some people's heads. When she got the cover feature of *The Face* magazine in February 1985, a male journalist gave her a hard time over the BOY TOY buckle. "That's a joke," she explained wearily. "It's a tag name given to me when I first arrived in New York... it's not for the women of the world, only for myself... It's a statement for innocent sexuality... BOY TOY is a *joke*."

At the beginning of 1985, Madonna the sex kitten began to blossom into Madonna the sex goddess. In the video for 'Material Girl' Madonna slipped out of her ethnic street rags into something far more sophisticated; an elegant pink satin cocktail dress and diamonds, just like the one that Marilyn Monroe wore in the film *Gentlemen Prefer Blondes*. Suddenly she was the archetypal Fifties' Hollywood blonde, reworking Monroe's classic 'Diamonds Are A Girl's Best Friend' scene. While on the cover of the single Madonna posed naked, kneeling on the floor and seductively clutching a blue satin sheet over her body.

Madonna said at the time, "My image is that I'm this brazen young woman who wears what

she wants and says what she wants... I guess I would be perceived as a sex symbol because I have a typically voluptious body... I love dresses like Marilyn Monroe wore, those fifties' styles really tailored to fit a voluptuous body. A lot of stuff made now is for an androgynous figure and it doesn't look good on me."

Not surprisingly, the press started to draw comparisons between Madonna and her heroine. It wasn't just the blondness and the beauty spot they shared, it was a natural affinity with the camera and "a vital, almost atomic capacity to project sexuality", which is how American *Life* magazine described Monroe in the fifties. Like Madonna, Monroe had also been a fascinating study in contradiction and paradox, with her strange mixture of bombshell promiscuity and sexual innocence.

"Madonna has the kind of face you want to look at blown up 50 feet high," said Susan Seidelman, director of *Desperately Seeking Susan*, Madonna's first major film. "She isn't conventionally beautiful but then neither were the Bette Davises or Marlene Dietrichs."

Desperately Seeking Susan was released in March 1985 and coincidentally saw Madonna playing a part that could have been written for her. Susan was a queen of street-style trash whose wardrobe mirrored Madonna's lace and rosaries, sun glasses, stockings and suspenders.

The following month, on her first concert tour, Madonna was amazed to see the overwhelming influence her style was having on American youth culture. Hundreds of thousands of young girls came to the concerts dressed just like her, with bleached and tousled hair, see-through tops, bras, fingerless gloves and crucifixes. Magazines and TV shows ran lookalike competitions and a new term was coined for Madonna clones – 'wannabes' – a word that was officially recognised in Webster's Dictionary in May 1991.

At first it was a mystery to Madonna why they would want to copy her look. "I never set out to be a role model. I am a strong woman, a successful woman, and I don't conform to a stereotype." Nevertheless she had been adopted as a symbol of sexual rebellion, and the reasons soon became clear.

"For so long young women have been told that there are certain ways they mustn't look if they want to get ahead in life," realised Madonna. "And there I was dressing in a forbidden way and yet obviously in charge of my life."

"You can wear all this stuff in the street nowadays, it's fine," said one wannabe when interviewed on television wearing lace and fishnet. "Madonna's the only one that we can look up to these days," said another. "When you wear Madonna clothes, everybody looks at you!" American rock magazine *Rolling Stone* put the Madonna phenomenon down to her accessibility. "She's not some perfect, unattainable sexual icon; she's a real person like her fans."

Above: The first Madonna image takes a recognisable shape... bangles, beads and a lion's mane of hair, the look she chose for the film 'Desperately Seeking Susan'.

Facing page: On stage during the first live tour... a ball of energy with crucifix and CND logo belt buckle.

Cycling shorts are perhaps the easiest item of clothing to copy from Madonna's wardrobe, worn with baggy T-shirt, trainers and baseball cap. But she also wears them as functional, modern-day bloomers under short skirts and dresses. Plain ones under a fancy tutu. Patterned ones under a plain dress.

Bold use of the visible midriff caught everyone unawares and helped Madonna towards stardom. She outdistanced her rivals in no time. The nude spreads which appeared in Penthouse and Playboy only increased interest.

"Most of all, I like Madonna when she is nude."
Jean Paul Gaultier.

Facing page: **Madonna at Live Aid, within days of the nude spreads appearing. 'I ain't taking shit off today,' she told the audience at Philadelphia. Indeed, she seemed overdressed for August.**

The American lingerie industry reported that their turnover was suddenly up by 40 per cent, and that Madonna's image was responsible for this underwear revival. "In the sixties women burned their bras, now they wear five at a time and bare their belly buttons," said one journalist. "Madonna has done for the corset and the crucifix what punk did for the safety pin," commented another.

Macy's New York department store devoted an entire 'Madonnaland' floor to selling her fashions, jewellery and posters, while official tour merchandise included the fingerless gloves and crucifix earrings.

One magazine article on 'The Invasion of the Wannabes' said, "America's stores, streets and schoolyards swarm with mimic Madonnas. The look has even filtered into the fashion fantasies of couture copycats in Paris; notably Christian Lacroix at the house of Patou, and Chanel's Karl Lagerfield."

Madonna's stage clothes were loud and colourful. She wore a sixties-style psychedelic miniskirt and jacket covered with bold, bright paisley patterns, CND symbols, and mock-diamond studded crucifix costume jewellery. Her 'Like A Virgin' wedding dress wasn't as daring as the one she had worn on her album cover, but it had a dramatic 20 foot train and was worn over a white midriff top with a gold crucifix logo, lacy leggings and lace-up boots.

"Madonna is a child-woman. She is fun and joyful, but she is also a femme fatale," said Maripol, the French designer who made the stage clothes for the tour. She operated a shop called Maripolitan in Greenwich Village, and business boomed while Madonna championed her goods.

In 1985, Madonna began to establish what would become an enduring reign of tartdom and terror as America's new 'It' girl, the term once used to describe Hollywood starlets who somehow struck a chord within the overall culture of their time. But Madonna was doing more than that. She was dealing a challenging blow to American middle-class morality, where the oh-so-touchy subject of sexuality always got brushed under the carpet in the unrealistic hope that it would go away.

Madonna's lacy underwear-as-outerwear was actually beginning to have an impact on the mood of society. Feminists accused her of setting women back 30 years, but they were missing the point. Madonna was nobody's BOY TOY and nobody's fool. On the one hand she wanted to see a return to fifties' values when women rejoiced in their femininity and weren't ashamed of their bodies; on the other she looked ahead to the Nineties when more and more women would take control of their own destiny.

"In our society a woman who is overtly sexual is considered a venomous bitch or someone to be feared," said Madonna. "So what I like to do is to take the traditional sort of overtly sexual bimbo

image and turn it around and say, 'You can dress this way or you can behave this way, but I'm in charge, I call the shots. I know what I'm doing'."

Madonna was breaking all the rules and setting her own boundaries. She argued that it was necessary to wear lingerie in order to feminise masculine qualities; to drive home the point that you could be sexy and strong at the same time. She cited Michael Jackson as an ally in her battle to break the mould of sexual stereotypes. "Michael Jackson isn't very masculine. He looks like Diana Ross. He has those beautiful doe eyes, he even talks like a girl and he's conquered the world."

Madonna's subversive antics provoked fiery debates in the press; many came down on her side. "Like Monroe, Madonna is bent on epitomizing and championing a certain vision of female sexuality, and like Monroe she is often damned and dismissed as an artist for doing so," said *Rolling Stone*.

"Like Mae West, Marilyn Monroe and Marlene Dietrich before her, Madonna almost mocks her femininity – which perhaps helps explain why she often incurs the wrath of feminists and has a large camp following, among others, from homosexuals," commented *The Observer*.

And Julie Burchill filled her pen from an inkwell of acid to write: "She is essentially a good thing as a role model... only the wimpiest New Man or Born Again Cow could deny that the best sort of girl is one who looks like a slut and thinks like a man, and Madonna has this in spades."

Bette Midler introduced Madonna at the Live Aid concert in Philadelphia in July 1985 as... "A woman who pulled herself up by her bra straps, and has been known to let them down occasionally." The infamous Madonna nudes, posed for in New York when she was broke and living on popcorn, had surfaced in both *Penthouse* and *Playboy* magazines in the same week.

The cover of *Penthouse* featured one of the raunchiest official shots that had been taken of Madonna at that time; wearing a midriff top with the word HEALTHY printed across her chest, and a clingy skirt hitched up around her thighs and down below her navel, Madonna tugged at the waistband of her tights and looked as if she was about to strip for the camera. While Madonna found publication of the nude shots a painfully embarrassing experience, in reality the pictures were rather tame. They were fairly innocent 'art' pictures, quite unlike the shots designed to cater to stereotype male erotic fantasies that are usually found in soft-core pornographic men's magazines. In the event they merely served to heighten her outrageous profile without damaging her already controversial image in any way.

In August Madonna married actor Sean Penn and wore a strapless wedding dress made from taffeta and chiffon, with a veil topped by a black bowler hat. Throughout their three-and-half-year marriage, Sean tried to temper Madonna's choice

The 'gamine' look. Short hair and child-like coquettishness, was originated by Shirley MacLaine and Audrey Hepburn during the fifties. Madonna hi-jacked the look for her 'Papa Don't Preach' video.

Madonna has never been afraid of her Italian ancestry. Crucifixes became part of her stage image. Here she pays tribute with a tongue-in-cheek T-shirt.

of clothes with caution. "Sean was very protective of me. He was like my father in a way. He patrolled what I wore. He'd say, 'You're not wearing that dress. You can see everything in that!'"

In 1986, just as the Disney studios decided to revamp Minnie Mouse's tired image with Madonna-style lace and jewellery, Madonna underwent her own metamorphosis. She was in a Monroe state of mind again, adopting a far more demure image for *Shanghai Surprise*, the critically savaged film she made with Sean Penn for former Beatle George Harrison's Handmade Films company. Gone was the wild child who would have been in danger of having 1985 stamped all over her. Now Madonna's make-up was pale and subtle. Her shoulder-length tresses were wavy and honey-blonde. She wore pretty thirties-style dresses and looked every inch the vintage movie queen.

"I see my new image as very innocent and feminine," she said, retaining the look for the video that accompanied her ballad, 'Live To Tell'. "In pop music, generally, people have one image. You get pigeonholed. I'm lucky enough to be able to change and still be accepted. If you think about it, that's what they do in the movies; play a part, change characters, looks and attitudes. I guess I do it to entertain myself."

By June, Madonna did a complete about turn by reinventing herself as a 'gamine', a type that had sprung up during the fifties with stars like Shirley MacLaine and Audrey Hepburn. Madonna's new impish short hair gave her a child-woman, urchin appearance. The gamine was the opposite pole of the sex goddess, and hinted at a new trend that was to keep cropping up in Madonna's career – her beloved flirtation with androgyny.

"I wanted to change my clothes. You wait for things to cool off. You wait for your image not to be plastered up everywhere. It goes in cycles. If you've got a product, you promote it. Obviously if you spend a couple of years wearing lots of clothes and tons of jewellery, and it just takes you forever to get dressed and your hair is long and crazy, then you get the urge to take it all off and strip yourself down and cut your hair all off just for a relief."

In the video for her controversial new single 'Papa Don't Preach', a song about teenage pregnancy, Madonna played the tomboy in jeans and black leather jacket, and a slogan T-shirt that announced ITALIANS DO IT BETTER. Alternating shots showed a sexier Madonna in a black bustier top and leggings – and there was something different about her body. It was less voluptuous and seemed more toned and muscular.

The full impact of her leaner physique was revealed in Jean Baptiste Mondino's video for 'Open Your Heart', in which Madonna played a peep-show stripper dressed in a short, dark spiky wig, fishnet tights and a bodysuit with tasselled

Brigitte Bardot's explicit sexuality has re-surfaced with a more studied edge.

The classic Marilyn Monroe look has been the most obvious influence on Madonna's wardrobe and Madonna has plundered the tragic star's taste in clothes from the 'Material Girl' period of 1985 to the present day.

Underwear comes out... courtesy of BB in the Fifties.

Madonna's heroines have one thing in common. Glamour. She has never been shy to take what she can from the Hollywood beauties of the past and even, at times, of the present.

INFLUENCES &

Right: Ann Margret, the star of numerous Hollywood hits. Combining her looks and figure with an all-round talent, she might have been a rival to Madonna had she been born two decades later.

Below: Other role models include Jane Fonda, who wore Sixties sci-fi corsetry for 'Barbarella'.

Above: The Supremes were Motown's best loved girl group. Growing up near Detroit, Madonna often wished she was black.

Far left: Greta Garbo, the silent screen's most sultry star, taught Madonna how to use her eyes in the art of seduction, a talent not lost on Breathless Mahoney in 'Dick Tracy'.

Centre left: Judy Holliday, whose scatter-brained screen image Madonna borrowed for her portrayal of Nikki Finn in 'Who's That Girl'.

Left: Marlene Dietrich's performance in 'The Blue Angel' was another sexual tour de force that influenced Madonna's style.

Left: Grace Kelly personified the cool beauty of the American rich, the kind of look Madonna adopted for her role in 'Shanghai Surprise'. It wasn't enough to save the film.

Far left: Jean Harlow's clinging dresses left little to the imagination and influenced Madonna's choice of costumes as Breathless Mahoney. The archetypal dumb blonde, Harlow oozed sex on and off screen.

HEROES/PART 1

cone cups; a foretaste of the daring stage style for which she was soon to become notorious.

For the cover of her *True Blue* album, photographer Herb Ritts captured perhaps the most flattering shot of Madonna that has ever been taken; an elegant profile in which she wears the palest of make-up (though as always, the reddest of lips) and tilts back her head to present the most swan-like neck since the one made famous by Audrey Hepburn. It was to become one of Madonna's favourite poses for the camera.

"Madonna has unlocked her pent-up yearnings for a glamorous image," declared glossy American magazine *Vanity Fair*. "She's been compared to almost every female from Cinderella to Barbarella."

In a series of stunning black and white photographs by Bruce Weber, this tiny shrimp of a girl appeared larger than life when she was featured in two prestigious American magazines – *Life* and *Vanity Fair*. Wearing glamorous gowns that reflected her more mature image, Madonna proved once and for all that you didn't have to be a flat-chested beanpole in order to make clothes look good.

"I probably look taller 'cos I've got such a big mouth... I have the little-person complex. People who are smaller are always trying to be bigger. I've been working on being big for so long."

Life put Madonna on their cover and ran the headline 'That fabulous couple, Madonna and the camera'. *Life* had always been an accurate barometer when it came to the world's hottest heroines; back in 1952 they had given Marilyn Monroe her first cover, when she too was an emerging star.

In *Vanity Fair*, Madonna posed naked with a sheet draped around her, revealing just her bare back, and looking like a statue of a svelte Greek goddess. "The hair is now soignée and platinum white. The belly is as flat as a board. The tarty look has softened to a cinematic siren's," commented the fashion journalist. "In the flesh she's lissome, compact, alert. She has lost that pubescent quality of puppy fat... her skin is translucently beautiful, gleaming with all the limelight it has soaked up."

Madonna told *Vanity Fair* about her exercise routine. Rising at six every morning (Madonna has always been an insomniac with little need for sleep) she would run for five miles or work out. She attributed her pale complexion to keeping out of the sun and eating a vegetarian diet.

In 1987, Madonna introduced a Spanish flavour to fashion when she wore a flamboyant flamenco dress in her video for 'La Isla Bonita', and later appeared on the cover of her *You Can Dance* album wearing a feminine toreador outfit with a lacy bustier, embroidered bolero, and a cummerbund with a flouncy bustle. The Spanish theme continued with some of the stage costumes for Madonna's Who's That Girl Tour, and the fashion market climbed aboard the Hispanic

bandwagon as off-the-peg boleros and tiered skirts appeared in every high street store.

But by far the most striking stage costume on the Who's That Girl Tour was Madonna's peep-show bodysuit and fishnet tights. In the year that had passed since she'd first worn that costume for the 'Open Your Heart' video, Madonna had honed her body to a surprisingly sinewy perfection.

Comparing before-and-after pictures of her first Virgin tour and the current tour left no doubt about the rigorous physical disciplines Madonna must have undergone to remodel her body. She has put her iron will down to her early days as a dancer when, "I realised that I could go from being unmoulded clay, and over time and with a lot of work and with people helping me, I could turn myself into something else."

If Madonna's life has been something of a Cinderella fairy tale, then her image has been an ugly duckling-swan transformation. Yet another stereotype had been smashed. While the majority of pop and rock stars from earlier eras had pushed their bodies to the limits by abusing themselves with alcohol, drugs and decadent lifestyles not unlike those of the royal families of ancient Rome, Madonna embarked on an obsessional love affair with health and fitness. She treated her body as a temple.

This she did with the help of her physical trainer, a blond Californian called Rob Parr. "When Madonna and I first met, she had a body that was in good shape, but she didn't have quite the definition. She was a little more voluptuous, a little softer in her arms, her legs, and in her upper body... I got her involved in a programme that strengthened her entire cardiovascular and muscular systems... one of the things that has really shocked people is to see the transformation in that period."

Newspapers started inventing Madonna diets while the flabby paparazzi gave chase as Madonna and her bodyguards went for their daily jog, a ritual she always maintains while touring. "I work out for two hours every day and have a huge dance studio and gym at home with weights, life cycles, a trampoline and a pool. I alternate my workout so it doesn't get boring. My trainer is a very well-rounded athlete and he really helped me get my shit together for my tour. I have a ten-speed bike and on alternate days I ride 25 miles up and down the hills along the Pacific Coast Highway, and I also run the stairs at Pepperdine University."

The Who's That Girl tour had the same title as Madonna's new film, in which she played the part of Nikki Finn, a streetwise woman wrongly convicted of murder. Madonna saw herself as a dizzy, screwball blonde, and tried to model her character on Hollywood starlet Judy Holliday. She wore comical ra-ra and tutu skirts with fishnet tights, and a glamorous Monroe dress for her love scene with actor Griffin Dunne.

Flanked by the ever present bodyguards, Madonna adopts the invisible look when jogging in the streets.

Facing page: **Madonna as belly dancer, her cameo role in the movie 'Bloodhounds Of Broadway'. The film bombed and has never had a general release in the UK, though it is available on video.**

Twin Peaks. *Madonna wore a stunning Dolce & Gabbana basque encrusted with glass beads to the première of her film In Bed With Madonna. In November 1991, Elle ran this fashion tip on how to copy the look. "Buy solid bras and sew on fringing, tassels, beads and bright stones, and wear with long evening gloves."*

A subdued brunette takes the curtain call after the first night of the play 'Speed The Plow' on Broadway in May, 1988.

Around the same time, Madonna did a light-hearted photo session with Alberto Tolot. Once described as sounding like "Minnie Mouse on helium" by *Time* magazine, Madonna literally took the Mickey by flirting with a giant Mickey Mouse toy. Wearing a black leather v-neck dress, and a tiny trilby hat fixed to one side of her head, she camped up the session by slipping Mickey's gloved hand inside her dress and feigning an admonishing glance. She also posed sitting in bed wearing Disney mouse ears and rolling her eyes to the back of her head.

Commented Julie Burchill, "Madonna got bored with being sexy; that is why she chooses to appear on magazine covers scowling grotesquely, wearing mouse ears and flexing her biceps. Being beautiful is now the smallest string to her bow... unlike more short-lived stars who seem to believe that the limelight is their birthright, Madonna works ceaselessly on being interesting."

Humour has always played a pivotal role in Madonna's overall style. Her tours have featured some over-the-top costumes that are a ludicrous blend of the sublime with the ridiculous: Dame Edna glasses, Mad Hatter hats with bunches of grapes dripping over the brim, and loud dresses covered with furry dice. Madonna then strips to reveal a sexy basque or bodysuit underneath. She plays the clown as well as she can play the siren, and her sex appeal has been described as both witty and intelligent. Her brother Christopher has said of her: "She's a comedienne, I think that's probably 99 per cent of what she's about - her sense of humour is really important. Most of what she does is based on that."

"My sense of humour may be the thing about me that is most misunderstood," says Madonna. "I don't take myself completely seriously. I laugh at myself in most of the things I do... it's like I start mocking the image that the public has of me."

Madonna once appeared on the American comedy show *Saturday Night Live* wearing a hooded sweat top, fur stole and sun glasses and announced, "Hi everybody, my name's Madonna and I'll be your comedy love slave for the evening." She then appeared in a sketch dressed as Princess Diana, convincingly attired in a regal satin gown, tiara and Di-styled hair.

Madonna thinks that a lack of humour is the death of anybody. "If you can't make jokes about yourself then you're not going to be happy. You'll be the saddest person that ever lived... you only have to have half of a brain in your head to see that I'm quite often making fun of myself. I mean, how obvious can I be?" Madonna even spices up boring business meetings with what she calls the 'suits', by... "walking in there with my orange velvet leggings and dropping popcorn in my cleavage and then fishing it out and eating it... I know I'm entertaining them, and I know that they know."

In 1988 Madonna recreated herself as a bru-

nette when she made her début on Broadway in a comedy play by David Mamet called *Speed-The-Plow*. Playing the part of a temporary secretary, she was hardly recognisable when she made her entrance wearing a modest suit, with newly dyed reddish-brown hair. "I felt kind of great having my own hair colour for the first time in years... I feel more grounded and Italian when I have dark hair, and I feel more ethereal when I have light hair."

Forced to live in New York during the play's run, Madonna befriended comedienne Sandra Bernhard and by night the pair trawled through the city's dance clubs, often dressed remarkably alike. Embroidered and patterned blue jeans cut-off just below or just over the knee, white T-shirts or spangled bras, peaked hats and tiny round sun glasses was the regulation wardrobe for their nights on the town.

In 1989, after a long musical absence, Madonna returned and reintroduced religion, bras, belly buttons and sex into her repertoire. In a photo session with Herb Ritts which appeared on the album cover for 'Like A Prayer', and in the March issue of *Rolling Stone*, she wore a mauve chiffon midriff top with a crucifix, blue jeans with beaded hippie belts, and colourful rings on every finger. Once again, fussy baubles, bangles and beads were the order of the day.

Just to be different, several pictures didn't even bother to show Madonna's face at all; they were cropped around her navel, which peeked out from an undone fly button. Head bowed in another shot, Madonna hitched up the hem-line of a long velvet dress to reveal a glimpse of stay-up stocking. Another picture showed her blowing smoke into her face as she held a cigarette in one hand, and grabbed her crotch with the other. Then, in the controversial video for her single 'Like A Prayer' in which she danced against a background of blazing crosses, Madonna wore lingerie; a simple slip as a dress, and a crucifix.

Madonna has said that she is never satisfied with who she is and that... "Change is important because it means that you've grown and it means that the life that you've lived and that you're living has affected you." But when Madonna was forced to take to the bleach again for her next film role as Breathless Mahoney in *Dick Tracy*, she admitted experiencing a slight identity crisis. "Being blonde is definitely a different state of mind... it has some incredible sort of sexual connotation. Men really respond to it."

Madonna responded to her blondness with complete sexual abandonment when she made the video for 'Express Yourself'. Shot with subtle lighting and in the best possible taste, she appeared naked and chained to a bed. A very feminine Madonna performed hip thrusts dressed in stockings and suspenders while a masculine Madonna slicked back her hair and danced in a double-breasted suit, grabbing her crotch and flashing her bra at the camera. And the monocle

Camouflaging flesh. *Many of Madonna's daring looks are strictly for the stage; modesty prevails on the street. Team hot pants with black leggings and high-necked tops. Wear skimpy dresses over matching Lycra T-shirts and thick, glistening tights. Even a basque or a body can be worn over a polo-neck top with thick leggings or tights.*

became a new fashion accessory when Madonna wore an old-fashioned eye glass around her neck.

The whole point of this expensive and extravagant exercise was to present two extreme images of women. "One is in charge, in control, dominating; the other is chained to a bed, taking care of the procreation responsibilities." For her next single 'Cherish' Madonna was a carefree gamine; with shorter hair and wearing a tight, wet dress, she flexed her biceps and swam with mermen in the sea.

In March 1990 Madonna made the sensational video for 'Vogue', the song that championed a curious underground New York dance craze called Voguing, the art of striking a dramatic pose. Self-conscious clubbers based their expressions and movements on old publicity shots of movie stars like Garbo whose plasticity of features enabled them to 'give good face'. With her bubbly blonde hair coiffeured into various period styles or dressed with wigs, Madonna mimicked her heroines in a video that both celebrated and laughed at such vanity.

It was at this point that Madonna finally took the see-through look of her early 'Virgin' days to its extreme. She had dispensed with the bother of wearing a bra underneath her lace top and, although her nipples weren't obviously exposed, many pop programmes saw fit to do some judicious pruning before the video was aired. Madonna also appeared naked from the waist up, crossing her arms in front of her chest and laughing; loving every moment. For those with a keen eye, she hinted at some of the new looks that could be expected on her impending Blond Ambition tour. There were shots of bizarre torpedo bras and lace-up corsets, and again, Madonna danced in a man's suit, worn open to reveal her bra.

As 'Vogue' went to number one all around the world, Madonna claimed the credit for making this obscure dance craze an international sensation. "It didn't make it before because it didn't have a spokesperson like me... I think it'd be great if everybody starts doing it. I love it because I think it has a lot of humour to it too. It's just so arrogant and presentational... I think it's hilarious."

Meanwhile, New York's high society were invited to a fashion show organised by *Vogue* magazine, and inspired by the Madonna look. Models trooped down the cat-walk wearing see-through lace tops, see-through lace wedding dresses, sequined bodices and large crucifixes. "I think that Madonna is a goddess of style for fashion," gushed André Leon Tally of *Vogue* magazine. "The force of her fantasy is accessible to everyone from 18 to 80." Some argued that Madonna was far less accessible now that she had lost her early amateurishness and chubby cuteness. Some even thought that her quest for a perfect body had resulted in her becoming a sexless, muscle-bound mutant.

On stage during the groundbreaking and controversial 'Blond Ambition' tour.

With Jean Paul Gaultier, who has been responsible for so many of Madonna's risqué outfits. Paris, October 1990.

"Jean Paul Gaultier is the man who stimulates Madonna's sex appeal. They are the perfect match – the outrageous fashion designer and the rock star with supermodel status."
Sunday Mirror, July 1990.

Madonna took her cue from 'Cabaret' for this section of the 'Blond Ambition' stage show. The ambiguous sexuality suited Madonna's style perfectly.

In April, Madonna appeared on the cover of *Vanity Fair* and posed for a fashion spread entitled White Heat, shot in a bar in Los Angeles. 'Getting into a new groove, the combustible star burns up Helmut Newton's lens' reads the introduction; a tribute indeed, since Newton is famed for his erotica.

A dramatic effect was ceated with Madonna's make-up. A pale, almost white foundation was applied to contrast with her bright scarlet lips, neatly pencilled eyebrows and shaded beauty spot. Her bubbly Breathless Mahoney hair looked several shades of platinum and gold.

In Newton's first shot, a wistful and immodest Madonna wears nothing but a necklace of real diamonds under a white plastic raincoat, belted tightly at the waist, with the collar folded back to partly expose her breasts. In the next shot, she abandons her cool composure and roars, open-mouthed with laughter, teasingly covering herself with her hands; first the siren, then the clown. Wearing a red Bob Mackie top with stockings and suspenders, Madonna is surrounded by male models in Armani suits; one aims a small dagger at her suspender strap, ready to cut it loose.

A scene from the film *Cabaret* is evoked as Madonna stands on top of a bar wearing a waistcoat, Gaultier bowler hat, and shorts over fishnet tights. Flashing her left breast, Madonna leers imperiously at a male onlooker seated beneath her, and waves a cane in his face. Laying demurely across a sofa on the next page, blue eyes staring seductively off-camera, Madonna wears a fragile, turquoise bodysuit by Giorgio di Sant'Angelo. Cut high above well-defined hip bones, it shows a great deal more 'leg' than any ordinary bikini line.

Stretching across the bar in a little black dress by Yves Saint Laurent, Madonna wears more diamonds and shows off her swan-like neck. And in a little white dress by Chanel that exposes a milk-white cleavage and bare, pale arms and legs, Madonna makes a ghostly vision as she sits astride a motorbike that's covered with a sheet.

The pictures in *Vanity Fair* were obviously a huge talking point. Five years ago, Madonna had been bruised with the humiliation of having her early nude shots plastered all over the pages of *Penthouse*. She flatly turned the soft porn magazine down when they offered her a million dollars to pose for a new, exclusive session. Yet now, voluntarily, she had stripped for a fashion shoot. Why?

Madonna had always considered the nude a work of art, and Newton was a master of erotica. These were pictures for posterity, and this time Madonna was in control of their release. But most of all, she was doing what she had always done best – seeking attention and sparking controversy – testing the parameters of public acceptance. Madonna simply enjoyed displaying her body, not for men, but for her own self-satisfaction. And this was no vacuous vanity, it was part of

High-waisted girdle-knickers *worn over fishnet tights evokes the Cabaret-meets-Clockwork Orange look that Madonna and Gaultier created for the Blond Ambition Tour. Team with a bowler hat and baggy cardigan.*

Madonna's defiant crusade to free the modern woman and her wardrobe from sexist interpretation. *Penthouse* had attempted to portray her as an object of desire, but now she portrayed herself as a woman of her *own* desire; proud of her body and secure in her femininity.

As Madonna's Blond Ambition tour kicked off in Tokyo, her autoerotic exhibitionism reached new heights – and found new expression – with coned torpedo bra tops, tight bustiers, suspenders and revealing corsets. These haute couture harlot creations were the handiwork of Jean-Paul Gaultier; outrageous designer darling of the pop world. Back in October 1989, in the middle of his summer collection, Gaultier had received a call from American photographer Herb Ritts, asking if he'd be interested in dressing Madonna for her tour. Having been an admirer for years, Gaultier couldn't believe his luck. "Since the beginning with 'Holiday' she was wearing tight clothes with a lot of jewellery, very interesting." comments Gaultier. "My clothes have always been in the same spirit as Madonna... I make always the same thing, corsets etc. She loves it. She'd worn some of my clothes before this."

"We collaborated on everything," remembers Madonna. "I sent him drawings originally of what I wanted. A lot of costumes were inspired by my stick drawings – I'm not a good artist – and then he threw his stuff in."

Gaultier was happy to let Madonna share the credit for the costumes. "The inspiration is from me and her," he agreed, "but first of all it's from her."

Gaultier flew to New York armed with 150 sketches he had made; Madonna's choice was impulsive and abrupt as she narrowed down the proposed designs to just half a dozen, commenting "Yes, I love it. No, I don't like it. Adorable. Too much. Not this. Yes that one."

"She is very easy to get along with," says Gaultier. "She doesn't change her mind like other people I've worked with... but you can't just tell her what to wear. I saw her with black hair and I told her it was great, but she prefers to be blonde. Madonna definitely knows what she wants."

The first fitting took place at Christmas in Paris. Later, when Madonna was in the middle of rehearsals, disaster struck; she had lost twelve pounds in weight. With just one week to go before the opening night, Gaultier and his team set to work on alterations. "The clothes were a bit baggy after that," he remembers, "But we rectified it. She was so slim before; where does she lose the weight from I wonder?"

The resulting outfits were erotic, exotic, and extrovert. Gaultier's bras and corsets were so extreme, they actually poked fun at the 'typical male' idea of female sexuality; reflecting the wicked sense of humour that he and Madonna shared. She had wanted the show to be a sexy mix of femininity and masculinity, spiced with the glamour of a Busby Berkeley musical, and spiked

INFLUENCES &

Aside from the obvious glamorous heroines that Madonna parades on stage, there are more subtle influences at work in the Ciccone mind. Here's a selection of the less obvious markers on the Madonna landscape.

Above *right clockwise:* Elizabeth Taylor in 'Cleopatra' perfected the art of the grand entrance; Shirley MacLaine, Louise Brooks and Audrey Hepburn personified the 'gamine' look that emerged in Madonna's little-girl-lost look adopted for the 'Papa Don't Preach' video.

***Right:* Liza Minelli won an Oscar for her portrayal of Sally Bowles in 'Cabaret', the musical based on Christopher Isherwood's stories of life in pre-war Berlin. Madonna lifted the look for her 'Blond Ambition' show... bowler hat, black stockings, suspenders and bustier.**

HEROES/PART 2

Left: Another tribute was the alternative 'Vogue' performance when Madonna utilised costumes worn in the film 'Dangerous Liaisons'.

'Carmen' was the image Madonna used for her performance of the Spanish song 'La Isla Bonita'. *Above:* Pola Negri in the 1918 film. *Left:* Laura del Sol in the 1984 version.

A cult Sixties TV show on both sides of the Atlantic, 'The Avengers' was first with the black leather cat-suit. After 25 years this action-woman style, zipped-up here on the young Diana Rigg, did not escape the attention of Madonna's designers.

Fishnet Fetish. *Madonna first made fishnet popular in 1983. In 1991 it returned to the catwalk; paraded by such haughty fashion houses as Chanel. Elle ran the following fashion tip in their November 1991 issue. "Chic, punky or plain sexy, fishnet returns as a basic body cover. Worn under a frayed denim skirt, as a revealing top under a long jacket (with or without a black bra) or as a flash of ankle under a pair of trousers."*

with the seediness of films like *Cabaret* and *A Clockwork Orange*. Inch by not-so-subtle inch, Madonna was testing those parameters again, and pushing them to their limits.

In the same way that the Catholic church had denounced the bikini when it became fashionable, now it denounced Madonna for the bustiers, bodysuits, swearing, and simulated sex that she touted on tour. But her crusade continued, and the once-constricting corset, a slavish, bone-ribbed symbol of female subjugation, now became a fashion statement. As for the bustiers, an influential Italian designer, expounding the virtues of the female bust, had this to say: "The bustier is an important symbol for us. The bust is the symbol both of maternity and sexuality. The bustier is a safety box half hiding something very potent which should only be opened in private."

Madonna made her dramatic stage entrance wearing a severe, ponytail hairpiece, her natural hair pulled back so tightly from her face, that the effect was like having a face lift. Too much bleach, it was rumoured at the time, was making her hair fall out. Madonna's first outfit was a black double breasted suit, with the jacket worn over – and the trousers worn under – a salmon satin bodysuit; pleated and embroidered with suspenders attached. Clever, slashed pockets in the jacket allowed Madonna's coned bra to peep through. It had taken Gaultier and his team three months of dedication and hard work to create such an eyecatching illusion of "masculine and feminine, suit and sex."

The illusions continued. A gold lace-up bodysuit with quilted cups and matching briefs; a striped and sequined circus basque with fringes; a black baby doll dress with a pink fur-trim; and Madonna's tribute to Liza Minelli – black bowler hat, black cage vest worn over a bullet bra, and velvet hotpants with fishnets and knee pads.

"I have never met anyone with such spark, such charisma. She is superb and surprising," enthused Gaultier. "Every minute of the concert where she dances, gesticulates, moves and changes costumes, she remains impeccable, never dishevelled, never shouting or crimson. Even fashion models don't possess this constant perfection."

The June issue of American magazine *Harper's Bazaar* ran a fashion spread with Madonna modelling some of her tour clothes, photographed by Jean Baptiste Mondino. On the cover she smiled a heavy-lidded smile, just like the one that Monroe had made so famous. Inside, she was introduced as 'The Cool Queen of White Heat Strikes Again'. In awe of Madonna's self-discipline the journalist remarked, "Just imagining this power-house breezing through her exhaustively documented daily régime is a wilting experience. It's clear that no one pushes herself harder than she, and that every drop of sweat shed in one area has its reward in another."

As well as her stage clothes, Madonna modelled a black vinyl jumpsuit with high-heeled, thigh-length boots; the kind of 'kinky' outfit Emma Peel would have been proud to wear in the sixties' series, *The Avengers*. English *Elle* magazine dedicated a whole feature on the return of 'bondage' as fashion, and the way it had changed from being a symbol of sexual repression, to a fashionable expression of personal pleasure and independence. "These clothes are modern armour - it's a look that is as threatening as it is alluring - moreover, it's about autoeroticism."

To illustrate the phenomenon, *Elle* ran pictures of Madonna in her cage vests and corsets; Jane Fonda as Barbarella, in her teasing, see-through, sci-fi bras; and the famous picture of a woman in a Mainbocher corset, taken by fashion photographer Horst P. Horst, and imitated by Madonna in her 'Vogue' video.

Fashion spreads showed the latest designs; lightweight easy-stretch satins and velvets transformed into corsets and corset dresses. *Elle* pointed out that bondage and fashion were not new bedfellows. In the fifties a lingerie mail order catalogue called Fredericks of Hollywood championed the 'movie star cleavage' by selling Wonder Worker bras with stitched-in, push-up pads. Fredericks of Hollywood was another strong influence on Madonna's stage clothes; they still sell lingerie, and needless to say, Madonna is one of their ardent customers.

"To many women there can be no objects more offensive, more heavy with symbolism and rife with male fantasy than the corset and high heels," said *Elle*. "But Jean-Paul Gaultier redefined the corset as modern and dynamic... this time around it's about fun and fantasy – assurance and choice. The public connoisseurs of this particular mode are Madonna, Grace Jones and Annie Lennox. Not for the meek and mild, their look is strident, daring and requires supreme confidence. It says 'I am in control of my sexuality and destiny.'"

French *Elle* magazine called Madonna 'the beast of fashion' and suggested ways to look like her with photographs of androgynous models wearing bizarre combinations of fishnet, sequins and suspenders. Madonna pulled a beastly, scowling face for the June cover of *The Face* magazine; an anti-glamour trend that continued with Herb Ritts's extraordinary black and white photo session for American *Interview* magazine. A short, black wig with a spiky fringe, and false, spidery sixties' eyelashes, transformed Madonna's appearance. She sneered menacingly at the lens and winked a lazy eye, with a cigarette held between her lips. On the cover, wearing a polka dot blouse, hotpants and bowler hat, Madonna mocked the classic macho Michael Jackson pose by presenting an image of woman that was all crotch and no subtlety.

Photographs from this session were also featured in Madonna's tour programme, in Italian *Vogue* magazine, and on the cover of her 'Immaculate Collection' album. One picture in particular caused a stir; Madonna posed inside a gentlemen's toilet, standing by a row of urinals wearing a basque with fishnets. In a dark, bobbed wig that made her look like another one of her heroines, actress Louise Brooks, Madonna bared her breasts again in a totally see-through blouse. In a cheeky corset she stood with her legs wide apart, laughed and leaned over, grabbed her breasts and pushed them up and out towards the camera. And a photo session by Patrick de Marchelier captured a butch Madonna giving 'attitude' in an unzipped leather jumpsuit, a heavy-lidded scowl half hidden under a leather cap, and a cigarette dangling from her mouth.

Commented Glenn O'Brien of *Interview* magazine, "Madonna has almost a kind of medium ability to read the minds of the audience and I think that she synthesizes everything that people are looking for in entertainment."

In July, Madonna's tour reached London and, as usual, the press stumbled along behind when she jogged in Hyde Park and followed her when she went shopping, documenting everything she wore. Walking around town surrounded by her enormous bodyguards, she didn't bother to put on much of a fashion show. Casual paparazzi shots of Madonna often show her walking the streets in cap and shades with scruffy hair and sloppy T-shirt belted outside clinging cycling shorts; confident enough to be caught looking obscenely 'normal'.

On her London shopping spree, however, Madonna bought the best that the city could offer in expensive South Molton Street. With her characteristic love of clothes that revived the spirit of the sixties, she bought a whole mix-and-match range by Florence's house of Pucci, the Italian designer who had revived psychedelia with his swirly-patterned, multi-coloured dresses, leggings and head scarves. Katharine Hamnett's store was closed to the public for Madonna's private inspection, while an assistant was sent to buy underwear from that great British institution, Marks & Spencer.

Running in England's absurdly tropical summer sun before each show, Madonna started a trend in anti-fur T-shirts with slogans like 'Your Mother has a fur coat? Mine lost hers' and 'Fur coats are worn by beautiful animals and ugly people.' Her strict vegan diet – allowing no dairy produce, meat or fish – was the subject of much press attention. Peter Chaplin, her Australian chef and dietician, cooked up healthy 'performance' foods with nutritious names like 'Fitness Noodles', 'Athlete's Answer' and 'Aerobic Apricot Curry'. Training food snacks consisted of rice cakes, nuts, grains, tofu and avocados. Madonna drank at least three litres of water a day, plenty of freshly-squeezed fruit juice, and only an occasional glass of wine.

"My job is to keep Madonna at her best fighting weight by eating the right things, and I never allow her to fall below 105 pounds," explained Chaplin. "These tours are terribly strenuous so

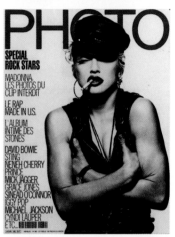

Madonna's ever changing face sold more magazines during the Eighties than any other American icon. Herb Ritts' shot of Madonna grabbing her crotch was much copied.

she needs endurance food. I give her slow-release carbohydrates like pasta and brown rice, and protein shakes made with soya milk... I let myself into her suite around 8.30 am to prepare breakfast, when she's just a tousled barefoot sleepy head, stumbling out to talk to me in her silk pyjamas."

After breakfast, Madonna would change into her tracksuit to begin a gruelling routine of sit ups, press ups, jumping, bending and stretching with body instructor Rob Parr. "Today we will run nine miles," said Parr at the time. "Her routine changes according to the country she's in and whether it's a show day. After our run we do an hour's aerobic conditioning, resistance training and stretch exercises. The most important muscles are the stomach. As well as her strong legs she has that beautiful 'v' the stomach muscles make when they are in perfect condition."

Not even a typhoon can stop Madonna in her tracks when she's training on tour. She travels with a portable gymnasium, and has been known to run the stairs of multistorey hotels – top to bottom – several times. "Madonna is serious about her body," confirms Parr. "She has a functional body and a functional body is sexy. I see her as a warrior, an Amazon in spirit. But at the bottom line, Madonna is a perfectionist."

"A lot of people say it's really sick," admits Madonna of the exercise obsession that keeps her vital statistics at a trim 34-22-33. "But my whole life is in a constant state of disarray, and the one thing that doesn't change is the work-out. If I had nothing to do, I would stay in the gym forever. It's a great place to work out aggression and depression – if you've failed in every way in your day, you've accomplished one thing – you've gotten through your work-out and you're not a total piece of shit."

Hot on the heels of the Blond Ambition tour came Madonna's new film, *Dick Tracy*. Set in the thirties and filmed in bold bright colours that attempted to recreate the look of the original cartoon strip, she played a nightclub singer called Breathless Mahoney who pours herself into the tightest of dresses, all slinky and strapless with plunging necklines and blatant sex appeal.

"I was wondering what a girl has to do to get arrested," runs Madonna's famous line in the movie.

"Wearing that dress is a step in the right direction," came Warren Beatty's famous reply. Beatty had a very definite vision of how he wanted Madonna to look in his film. He collaborated with costume designer Milena Canonero to create her sexy screen image, while Madonna worked on specific exercises for her upper body, in order to regain her once-voluptuous curves.

The thirties had been a golden age for sensual fashion; sleek, clinging creations worn by Hollywood stars like Jean Harlow and Marlene Dietrich. Moulded to women's bodies like second skins were satin evening gowns that demanded

With Warren Beatty at the Washington première of 'Dick Tracy' in the summer of 1990.

Facing page: **Madonna's off-duty look usually reflects the American preoccupation with physical fitness and her own desire for anonymity, even when she's out clubbing.**

"The only time Madonna isn't sexy is when she jogs in baggy T-shirts and leggings. But the motive is sexy – regular running sessions give her the Body Beautiful."
Sunday Mirror, 1990.

A VOGUE'S

Is it fair to say that Madonna brought femininity back into fashion?

Yes, and it was in quite a shocking way. Fashion had been very androgynous, there had been a lot of cross dressing before she came along. I think essentially what she did was add the idea of *power* to femininity. Before, women had steered away from looking feminine because we'd thrown the baby out with the bathwater. We didn't want to look like women because we associated everything to do with femininity to be connected with powerlessness, weakness, vulnerability and not being taken seriously. So there was a huge denial thing going on, and Madonna shocked by empowering those rejected ideas of femininity.

Sarah Mower, Associate Editor and Beauty Director of British Vogue Magazine talks about how Madonna has brought femininity back into fashion, Madonna's role in reviving lingerie and whether Madonna's example panders to age-old male fantasies.

Was Madonna responsible for reviving the lingerie industry?

Not single-handedly; the underwear-as-outerwear phenomenon is not something that she invented. Jean Paul Gaultier is the person that has to be credited with that; he's been doing the bra in all kinds of exaggerated guises since about 1984. And even earlier, in about 1981, Vivienne Westwood put huge satin bras on top of jumpers and everyone thought 'This is Vivienne going mad!' I asked Vivienne about that once and she said that it was Malcolm McLaren who actually thought of that idea, so perhaps you have to hand it to him.

It's interesting to ask how original Madonna has been from a British point of view, because the young British people have been so inventive in their dressing. And if Madonna is taking from Gaultier, then Gaultier is taking from British street fashion. He admits that openly; that he's been coming to London and buying clothes from Camden market to see how people put things together, going back to Paris and turning it into expensive fashion, then selling it back to the kids. Underwear-as-outerwear really goes right back to punk. So maybe you can't credit any designer with it.

Madonna isn't a designer. She knows how to use ideas, she doesn't necessarily invent them. But for any idea to become an acceptable trend, you need a famous person to be seen wearing it, otherwise fashion is only seen on the catwalk and everyone says, 'Who the hell would wear that?'

EYE VIEW

Fashion editors still argue about the morality of corsets, suspenders and bras. Is female fashion pandering to male fantasy, or is the joke on the men?

I think we're pandering to our *own* fantasies. We've reached a stage where women feel they've got to a point of equality with men. We look at men and say, 'Actually we don't want to be men. We don't want to wear those suits. We don't want to be as hard and as one-dimensional as them. We are women, therefore we want to wear womanly clothes'. And that's the whole area that Madonna goes into, the area of 'what exactly is gender?'

It doesn't set women back because we're not saying that we want to be like our mothers and grandmothers were in the Fifties. You can't turn the clock back like that. And it definitely *is* having a laugh at men because they get helplessly turned on by it – and more fool them really!

Madonna is definitely saying that woman is in control. It needs someone as strong as her to wear those clothes and say it. You only have to look at Kylie Minogue to realise that she's parroting the same beliefs and it doesn't necessarily work. Can you really believe that Kylie is anything other than a pretty, rather straightforward little Australian girl?

Has Madonna set new standards of beauty?

Oh yes, the whole importance of the way she keeps changing her look says to men that there's no one absolute ideal of beauty, and that you can be what you want to be by changing X, Y and Z. It's in your own hands. You are your *own* Barbie doll to play with, rather than being an object.

I met her once in 1984 when 'Lucky Star' was in the charts and I couldn't have told you then that she was going to be a mega-star. She was attractive and had good skin, but her face and features are not classically beautiful and she knows that.

The transformation she's been through has given women possibilities. The important thing from the point of view of hair and make-up is that she's made some artifice possible. Before, in the Sixties and Seventies, a woman was just supposed to be a beautiful 'chick' and it all had to look natural. You had long, flowing hair, the colour that you were born with; if you wore make-up you tried to make it look as if you didn't wear make-up. And Madonna brought back this whole thing of dyeing your hair and being obvious about it; being a brassy blonde and wearing a lot of make-up, and changing the look of your face. That's brought out a huge revival in hair and make-up fashions. When she had her lip done (with collagen), it went against her ethos in that she isn't obviously very unhappy about her upper lip!

Has Madonna changed the fashion ideal of the female figure – from being skinny to being shapely and strong?

You have to remember that the aerobics and fitness cult has been around for the whole of the last decade. A lot of people think Madonna's gone too far with it. Warren Beatty made her put weight on for *Dick Tracy* and he was right, she looked great in that film.

I don't think it's healthy to make girls feel they have to work out the whole time. You can't have a perfect body. If you're thin, you don't have bosoms and probably if you're muscular you don't have bosoms either, so you can't have it all! There are areas in which Madonna is a very liberating force – and other areas where she's just a victim of her time.

What will Madonna have to do to stay on top?

I've got a sense that the underwear thing is all going to be over quite soon. What Madonna will have to do next is prove that she can be something beyond that. She knows only too well that you're only as good as your next look. Once everybody's copying you, it just becomes too accessible. If you're a leader you have to lead, and the only way to do that is to turn your back on it. There's a definite move towards more lady-like dressing and since Madonna's so interested in fashion it will be interesting to see whether she can personify a lady-like person or not.

Thus far she's brought femininity back in a very, very ironical way, it can be read on so many different levels, and in a very, very un-American way, because Americans don't usually understand British irony and sarcasm. But the age of blatant sexuality is fast proving to be very passé. Once we start moving into a new age, there's going to be a new look on the horizon – although there seems to be a bankruptcy of ideas among fashion designers at the moment. As long as Madonna can rise above that counter-cultural thing she's so deeply into – I think you can probably trust her to be the first to find it.

Madonna staged her own 'Dangerous Liaisons' style cabaret for her alternative version of 'Vogue', first seen at the 1990 MTV Awards. Her 18th Century costume came complete with beehive wig and fan. At one point her dancers took hold of her breasts and crawled inside her skirts.

tight unobtrusive corsetry or a naturally slim figure; no tell-tale bulges were allowed to mar the streamlined effect.

Madonna has since complained that... "the dresses took more fittings than I had shooting days in the movie... my worst fault is impatience. Nothing goes as fast as I want it." And then there were problems with design. Tempers flared when Madonna argued that she could neither breathe nor move in some of the skin-tight gowns. Beatty had promised to make Madonna look great in this film – and some comfort had to be sacrificed in order to achieve Breathless's bold and brassy image.

The chairman of Walt Disney Studios, who released the picture, acknowledged the genius of Madonna's own image; her ever-surprising metamorphosis as a trend-setter. "She's always evolving; she never stands still. Every two years she comes up with a new look, a new way of presenting herself, a new attitude, a new act, a new design. And every time it's successful!" he enthused. "There is this constant 'genesis'. When something like that happens once, maybe it's luck. Twice is a coincidence. Three times it's just remarkable talent. A kind of genius. And Madonna's on her fifth or sixth time!"

In September Madonna wowed everybody at the American MTV video awards when she presented an alternative version of 'Vogue', dressed in French 18th-century aristocrat costume. She wore a dress from the film *Dangerous Liaison*, complete with period beehive wig and fan, while her male dancers wore shorts with their satin shirts and waistcoats. It was a bawdy and bodice-ripping performance; Madonna allowed her dancers to grab hold of her breasts and crawl up inside her skirts; at one point she flashed her white stockings, suspenders and bloomers at the audience, who roared with spontaneous approval. Curtsying graciously at the end, she was carried off lounging upon a regal sofa, peering at the crowd through a pair of opera glasses.

In November the BBC bestowed something of an accolade upon Madonna by dedicating a serious documentary to her, an episode of *Omnibus* entitled 'Behind The American Dream'. Exalting her as a 'sexual icon', they gave fair warning that 'the programme contains material and language of an explicit nature which some viewers may find offensive.' Indeed it did.

Madonna's subversive effect on culture was explored at great length. The BBC's cameras trailed a Madonna wannabe who had turned her obsession into a full time career by becoming a professional lookalike. At Harvard University in Massachusetts they filmed a professorial seminar on the subject of women in popular culture, during which students discussed Madonna's belly button and the nature of her erotic appeal. On a car radio they tuned into the reverential banter of an American DJ who gushed, "Madonna is achieving one of the attributes of the divine – omnipresence – the woman is achieving near-mythic proportions!"

In a monologue to the camera, shot in black and white at Madonna's request and looking very 'Sixties' as a result, she admitted that all this adulation sometimes made her feel insecure. "Sometimes I don't know who I am, but it doesn't have so much to do with me changing, as it's about having your own image and your face and your personality being made larger than life, and in a way dehumanised. So that when that happens I look at me and I say that's not me – *I'm* me."

Madonna wore a blonde wig for her interview; long and straight with a centre-parting. And her lips looked strangely fuller than usual. There was gossip at the time that she was having collagen treatment, which involved regular injections of a substance taken from cows' tails. A 'spokesperson' denied the story and said that Madonna was simply applying her make-up differently. But close-ups of Madonna on *Omnibus* left no room for doubt: her strangely swollen lips were the result of something more powerful than lip liner.

In November the MTV video channel shied away from Madonna's forwardness when they banned her shocking video for 'Justify My Love'; an orgy of semi-nakedness and stylish eroticism, directed by Jean Baptiste Mondino. Stripping down to her scanty underwear, Madonna almost made love to her current boyfriend Tony Ward, watched by a host of disturbingly androgynous characters in bondage gear. While the daily papers ran headlines that condemned Madonna for plumbing the depths of bad taste, several style magazines ran features that hailed Mondino as one of the world's greatest controversial image gurus.

"I've worked with Madonna a few times now," said Mondino referring to his peep show video for 'Open Your Heart' and photographs for *Harper's Bazaar*. "There's more to her than people think. She's a great actress. So I wanted to do something less glamorous, less slick, more real."

Naturally, the video sparked intense debates about Madonna's motives for making such a torrid adult fantasy. She had certainly ended the new decade with a bang. In a feature in *Esquire* magazine that explored 'a journey through the male experience' from the forties to the nineties, the writer observed, "In our role models, our heroes, our leaders, our objects of desire, the transformation has been extraordinary, if not spectacular. Consider the distance between Vera Lynn and Madonna."

Brushing aside her critics Madonna commented, "It's flattering to me that people take the time to analyse me and that I've so infiltrated their psyches that they have to intellectualise my very being. I'd rather be on their minds than off... I guess I just have a sense of mischievousness... you can take what I do at surface value or you can go underneath the surface. I don't want to be pigeonholed."

In 1991 Madonna mixed glamour and controversy with her new photo session for the April issue of *Vanity Fair*. A pin-up portfolio of pictures by Steven Meisel paid homage to Marilyn Monroe and Madonna's uncanny likeness to her. Entitled 'The Misfit', the introduction made the point that, like Monroe, Madonna was 'becoming increasingly isolated behind her white-heat fame.'

Laying on a blue rug in a fluffy lavender sweater; shoehorned into slinky Norma Kamali dresses; and posing completely naked; Madonna's expression captured the same poignant air of tragedy that so often appeared in shots of Monroe. The likeness had never been more astounding. In one shot, Meisel got Madonna to pose semi-naked behind a flesh-coloured piece of gauze, in imitation of a famous Monroe portrait taken by Bert Stern in 1962, just two months before she died of an overdose aged 36. Madonna was four years younger and a fighter.

"I don't see myself as Monroe," said Madonna. "I'm always playing with her image and turning it around. It's the idea of using imagery people understand, but having a different message. What I am saying is not what she was saying... she was made into something not human in a way, and I can relate to that. Everyone was obsessed with her sexuality and I can certainly relate to that."

Madonna also modelled an original Monroe costume; a pretty, patterned blouse and black

satin skirt from the film *Bus Stop* made in 1956, in which Monroe played a saloon singer called Cherie. But the shot to beat them all was a softly focused, double page nude spread, in which Madonna lay upon a mattress that was covered with Ralph Lauren designer sheets, tucked surreptitiously here and there to retain a sense of modesty. Just when you thought it was safe to assume that Madonna had taken her controversial image as far as it could go – she unveiled her pale pink birthday suit for *Vanity Fair*. (Although actress Demi Moore outdid her in the August issue by posing both naked and pregnant.)

"Madonna has no equal at getting attention," commented actress-turned-writer Carrie Fisher, in a frank interview with *Rolling Stone* a few weeks later. "She often seems to behave like someone who has been under severe restraint and can now say and do whatever she likes without fear of reprisal. She delights in being challenged... in going further than she had intended... there is no 'too far' for Madonna."

Feeling compelled to try and understand the motives behind Madonna's never-ending need to shock, Carrie put it to her: "Sometimes it seems like you have the attention of the world and sometimes you behave as though you don't. It's like you haven't caught up with the reality."

"It's not something I sit around and think about," replied Madonna. "It's rather unconscious... it's like pulling the table-cloth off the table to disarm everybody."

Mad Hatter. *Madonna makes great use of flamboyant hats and wigs to create new illustrations, while feathers, fishnet and high heels are favourite accessories. The result is a curious mixture of drama and frivolity.*

Facing page: For the 'Dangerous Liaisons' 'Vogue' sequence, Madonna hired an actual costume used in the film.

Femme Fatale. *Madonna knows that nothing looks sexier on a girl than a trouser suit. Express yourself with a man's classic pinstripe suit, or more feminine trouser suit, worn with a bustier or bra.*

Madonna's unlikely liaison with Michael Jackson never seemed likely to develop, either professionally or personally. All it did was grab headlines for a few days. Afterwards Madonna admitted that her attempts to remodel him fell on deaf ears: she wanted to cut his hair Caesar style.

At the 63rd Oscar awards ceremony in Los Angeles, movie moguls watched open mouthed as Madonna pulled off a saucy strip-tease stunt. She took to the stage, peeling off one of her long gloves and tossing aside her stole to reveal a Hollywood dress and a movie star cleavage. Designed by Bob Mackie, the shimmering, sequined, hourglass gown made Madonna look voluptuous again; so much so that *The Sun* newspaper was convinced that she must have had implants. They ran one of their classic front page headlines, on this occasion a spoof of *'Ello 'Ello*, the TV French Resistance farce: MADONNA WITH THE BIG BOOBIES - HAS SHE HAD OP UP TOP?' They even went to the trouble of showing pictures to a Harley Street plastic surgeon who inevitably said, well, yes – he supposed it was *possible*.

Michael Jackson made a surprising partner for Madonna at the Oscars, firing rumours of one of Hollywood's strangest ever couplings. The two were later seen dining out together, and were said to be working on a secret musical project. Madonna had always been intrigued by Jackson's asexual persona, but for the two of them to be romantically linked seemed like trying to get the lamb to lay down with the lion. She once commented that she could never take Jackson seriously when he kept grabbing his crotch because... "I feel that he's a very androgynous person and I don't believe him."

Now, Madonna couldn't resist the challenge of trying to pull Jackson out of his closet, revamp his image and make him believable. She had issued him with an ultimatum: "I said, 'Look Michael, if you want to do something with me you have to be willing to go all the way'... I would like to completely re-do his whole image, give him a Caesar – you know, that really short haircut – get him out of those buckled boots and all that stuff... I keep telling him 'I'd love to turn my two gay lead dancers on you for a week. They'd pull you out of the shoe box you're in'." At the end of the day, however, Jackson not surprisingly shied away from such drastic measures and Madonna had to concede, "This guy doesn't need me. He knows what he wants."

In May a party was thrown in New York for the première of Madonna's new film, *Truth Or Dare* (called *In Bed With Madonna* in the UK), a tell-all documentary filmed during the Blond Ambition tour. Madonna showed up for the party as a born-again brunette. She had dyed her hair dark brown because continuous use of bleach had become a painful process and was taking its toll on her hair. "My chapters in my life don't begin with the colour of my hair," she told the press. "I suppose it is really a new chapter in my life because now I'm finally finished with the movie. This is kind of my farewell to it." She also wore one of her most eye-catching costumes yet, a black satin robe worn open to show off a skimpy, spangled, multi-coloured basque with matching

Marilyn Monroe's wardrobe has been a huge influence on Madonna's taste in clothes. Here Madonna models a sparkling off-the-shoulder gown similar to that worn by Monroe in 'Gentlemen Prefer Blondes'.

jewellery and black stay-up stockings.

In a promotion shot for the film, Madonna stands with her back to the camera, wearing only a pair of unzipped hotpants, and the words ALL ACCESS scrawled upon her back; indicating the intimate nature of the backstage footage captured by film-maker Alek Keshishian.

Madonna went to the 44th Cannes Film Festival to promote the film, and she succeeded in disrupting the tediously stilted proceedings by pulling the red carpet from under everyone's feet without any apparent effort. Her outrageous costumes and behaviour stole the show, injecting new life into an event that had long lost its sparkle, and she attracted more press attention than all the other celebrities gathered in Cannes put together. Not since the gay and glamorous fifties had there been so much posing and partying beneath the swaying palm trees. Madonna and her entourage booked themselves into the Riviera's most exclusive Hotel Du Cap at Eden Roc, with Madonna herself occupying the palatial pink Princess Suite.

After allowing anticipation to mount for a day or two, she scored the biggest publicity coup in the history of the festival with a Cleopatra-style entrance into town, and another cleverly orchestrated strip-tease. With her dark hair curled and piled up on top of her head, and wearing a long shocking-pink satin gown pulled across her body, Madonna looked as if she had stepped straight out of the opera Madam Butterfly. Shedding the gown, allowing it to drop to the floor, she stood in nothing but her underwear; a white satin conical bra and matching panty-girdle hotpants. The crowd went wild as she wiggled her bottom at the cameras, but there were mixed reactions in the press. Some thought Madonna's hijack of Cannes should cause France to hang its head in shame, while others toasted her cheeky bravado: "Long live Madonna! Long may she reign in her pointed bras."

Said Robert Sandall of *The Sunday Times*, "You could feel her presence – or the reflected glare of her celebrity – at a distance of 20 miles... everyone was talking about the only real star in town – Madonna."

"No one could ever beat her in the self-promotion game," acknowledged the *Daily Express*. "There will only be one big show in town... snake-like, the Material Girl has, for seven years, shed the skin of one image after another until, finally, it has become difficult to distinguish her reality from her fiction."

And a disgusted veteran producer grumbled: "It's disgraceful. This woman has made just four films, two of which have been absolute bummers, and she takes over the festival... all the other stars will feel just like extras and their films will seem like supports to her main feature."

And indeed, little news of anyone else filtered through. The papers were full of pictures of Madonna jogging and parading outlandish new outfits, such as her comical and fashionable Gaultier tutu suit; a grey dinner jacket worn with a matching tutu skirt, black hotpants, white stay-up stockings, lace-up ankle boots, and pearls. Said Madonna of the whole event, "It was a real thrill, it was great, I felt like I was going to be crowned or something."

In June 1991, it was finally official – corsets, basques and hotpants were mainstream fashion thanks to Madonna. "Imaginative designs and modern stretch fabrics bring a new lease of life to a once restrictive garment," enthused *Elle* magazine over the corset. While *The Observer* magazine ran an article on 'Curve Queens' using photos of Hollywood starlets like Jane Mansfield and Marilyn Monroe who first championed this 'body-conscious' fashion. "Paris is all atremble with models strutting their stuff in girdles and spiked heels. Curves are back and the corset is in. But the new body-conscious dressing is about fitness and strength as well as femininity; the nineties silhouette was born in the gym and the nineties woman chooses her image."

The old debate continued - wasn't all this lingerie a backward step? Weren't corset-style dresses, girdle skirts, boned tops and underwired bodies relaunching women as mere bimbo objects of male desire? *The Observer* came down firmly on Madonna's side, arguing that this time the joke was on the men. "For Madonna they're attention-seeking stage clothes. For the rest of us they're a further stage of body-conscious dressing... although she receives criticism – and envy – the woman who dons the whole corset caboodle, not in but outside the boudoir, will counter that it is a celebration of women by women."

Cheeky hotpants were another crucial summer item for those who 'chose' to flaunt it. Said one magazine "Twenty-one years ago hotpants hit the headlines. Praised, reviled, whistled at, denounced – they were the fashion fad you couldn't ignore. Now they're back."

In the June issue of *Rolling Stone*, Madonna took body-consciousness to new extremes when she and photographer Steven Meisel collaborated on a portfolio of pictures entitled 'Flesh Fantasy'. Together they recreated the sexual underworld of Paris in the twenties and thirties, with its secret night-life of brothels, cabarets, and gay and lesbian nightclubs, evoking images from 'the erotic theatre of the imagination.'

Said Madonna, "For me, it was a great chance to re-create an era that I feel I would have really flourished in, that nothing I would have done would have been censored." On the cover, against the backdrop of a pink satin curtain, Madonna the brothel girl sits astride a chair wearing nothing but stockings, suspenders and high-heeled shoes. Inside she poses as a lingerie-clad contortionist; rudely perched on a chair with her legs apart in the air, drinking from a glass held between her feet; poking out her tongue and straining forward

The 'Flesh Fantasy' portfolio in the June 1991 edition of 'Rolling Stone'. The same issue carried a sexually frank interview with Madonna by actress Carrie Fisher.

Bold New Looks. *September 1991, Elle magazine lists Madonna as one of today's strong women in a feature called 'Bold New Looks' (along with the likes of Scarlett O'Hara, Frida Kahlo, Dolly Parton and Sinéad O'Connor). "Beauty has acquired a new strength, a new certainty. Self-assured baldness reflects women's changing attitudes to beauty and to themselves...the idea of a strong Amazonian woman is considered to be a turn-on rather than something repulsive... Make-up is no longer about hiding your insecurities, but about celebrating individuality, womanliness and strength." Readers are advised not to disguise their natural features, but to emphasise them. "Take note of your skin tone, eye and hair colour, and the strength and balance of your features ...make a statement about yourself."*

MAKING-UP NIGHT&DAY

Madonna has undergone an incredible transformation over the years; from a post-punk Cyndi Lauper lookalike, with shaggy eyebrows and messy, back-brushed hair, into a really classy act. It was as if somebody took her aside and said 'Okay, you've had your fun, now let's make you a star'.

She went from streaked hair to platinum blonde. All the Hollywood stars women admired and tried to copy were blondes. Stars with dark hair never became 'idols' like Madonna.

Her hair changes a lot. There are more hair changes than make-up changes. She's lucky in that she can carry off any hair colour without having to rethink her facial image. But it can't be easy for her to sustain dark hair with her lifestyle because – if you're tired and pale – you can look like death warmed up with dark hair. But blonde will always look stunning. It's easier to look good every day.

Madonna has a heart-shaped face, which means her cheek-

Top make-up artist *Katya Thomas* takes a tour around Madonna's face and reveals the secrets of her uncommon beauty. Follow her steps to achieve the look.

bones automatically follow a line – everybody wants those high cheek-bones! She has a very pointed chin, which looks good in photographs because you've got the wide eyes – which are always the focal attention of the face – and then you're drawn in with this pointed chin, down to the mouth and the beauty spot.

Sometimes she hides her beauty spot and paints one on her cheek. This is done to draw your attention to her eyes instead. Her nose is strong and very straight. Some people have a real one-look face, whatever you try to do with make-up, but Madonna has the kind of face than can project different illusions.

She has very small lips, and lines them to give them a more definite shape. She experimented with collagen treatment to make them bigger, but didn't go for a second dosage because she realised it wasn't good for her nose shape. Her upper lip looked far too close to her nose. She usually wears dark lip colour. Lighter colours would actually make her lips look fuller, but they say that all powerful women wear red lipstick because they want to be taken seriously.

There are so many different shades of red lipstick on the market, and you have to choose the one that suits you. People don't realise the colour tones in red lipstick; it's either blue – which is cold – or a true 'orange' red – which is warm and flattering. Madonna uses a true pillar-box red; it's very Forties.

Madonna's eyes are her strongest feature by far, almond-shaped with really well-set lids that roll back into the skull, giving good socket definition, and such a

depth and intensity to her face. She's got blue-grey eyes and brings out the blue in them with brown eyeshadow. Nothing brings out blue like brown eyeshadow! The extreme of that tone would be the golds, which she also uses.

She uses eyeliner next to her lashes; an eyeshadow used as eyeliner for a natural effect, or pencil for a harder look. She's got very long lower lashes and emphasises them by applying mascara, although she often wears false eyelashes.

Eyebrows are so important to Madonna's look. They're plucked and tidied up, but when she first came along she had those thick, shaggy eyebrows that were so fashionable at the time; everybody was growing their eyebrows as big as they could and brushing them straight up. Now the fashion is for a really strong Forties' Hollywood shape. Madonna defines her eyebrows so that they're thicker towards the middle and finer towards the outside. They've got a good natural arch. She darkens them with eyeshadow for a soft, natural look, and with pencil for a more dramatic feel. She brushes them up, following the direction that they're naturally growing in.

Sometimes she goes for a Sophia Loren look by making her eyebrows squarer. The stronger she gets with her make-up, the squarer she gets with her eyebrows. This

gives the face a real lift; the higher everything looks, the younger you look.

She always highlights under her eyebrows. Highlighting the brow-bones makes the sockets look deeper and makes the eyebrows jump out. The stronger her eye make-up gets, the whiter her highlighter gets. Peach is used for a more subtle illusion.

Eyebrows, eyeline and red lipstick are the three essential ingredients to Madonna's look, and this dramatic make-up looks best with pale skin. Her skin has quite an ordinary, scrubbed look. The colours that she uses are all neutral tones. It's a very clean look; she must have to dash off to the loo every five minutes to check it!

Madonna is very aware of herself in total. The best flirts in the world are extremely body conscious. She has a strong face and knows how to use it; just the way she raises an eyebrow can have such an impact.

A good trick Madonna uses for a no-fuss, instant make-up is to wear dark glasses with red lipstick. She still draws in her eyebrows and a hard, black eyeline to lift up the eye, but there's no need for eyeshadow. It's a real 'Hey I'm a star!' look. She really goes for the Hollywood imagel She's obviously an avid fan of old movies and gets a lot of ideas from her screen idols.

I ought to mention that I think Madonna does the best armpit shaves I've ever seen. Every time you see her armpits in a video, she's just got the closest shave – I expect she probably has them waxed.

NIGHT...

You can really go to town with this look. The secret is to 'go for it!' but keep everything really clean; so that the result is truly professional. Madonna uses a lot of hair-pieces and wigs; experiment for a special occasion.

5.
Using a matt, ivory shadow (white would be too harsh) highlight the area over the bone just under the eyebrow, where it starts to narrow.

6.
Sweep ivory shadow over inner lid area and along next to lashes, leaving outer lid area free.

4.
Use a black or brownish black eyeliner pencil and scribble a little of it onto back of your hand. Using a fine brush and a little dark brown shadow, mix on back of your hand and use to darken brows. Keep shape strong and definite—start gently and stop to check results as you go. Keep to a fine edge at the outside and emphasise with extra length.

7.
Choose a matt, mid-brown or grey shadow and blend in the outer lid area, up towards the brow. Blend into an almost invisible cover.

8.
Using a matt, dark brown or grey shadow, sweep a line of colour along socket line. Don't follow the line down; stop short just before and blend a little upwards to create a widening effect.

1.
Choose a fairly pale foundation; aim to look 'interesting' rather than anaemic! Tip a little onto back of hand and apply to the face with a cosmetic sponge. Start in the centre and sweep outwards, blending away into jawline and hairline. Coverage should be just a little heavier than the day-look, so skin looks perfect.

9.
Paint an extra-fine line along top of lashes using traditional eyeliner, felt-pen eyeliner, or matt black eyeshadow with a fine brush and a little water. (Pencil would be too thick.) The eyeline should taper up and out; the end flick should suit your own, individual eye shape.

2.
Hide any blemishes with a concealer that is slightly lighter than the base. Pat with fingertip. Use concealer under eye area, only where the line of shadow appears, and pat with fingertip.

10.
Apply false eyelashes if desired, joining them where your real lashes join the eyelid. Repeat eyeline when glue has dried, to conceal the join.

3.
Apply loose, translucent powder with a powder puff, with a firm pressing-and-rolling action. Use a small flat brush to powder around nose creases and over entire eye area. Brush off excess with a large brush in downward strokes.

11.
Apply two coats of black mascara, taking care not to clog.

13.
Line the lips and fill in the shape with a red pencil. Blot with tissue paper. Apply a matt, bold-red lipstick with warm tones, taking it over to the edge of the lipline to avoid a hard, pencilled outline. Blot, dust with loose powder, and apply a final coat of lipstick.

14.
Dot a beauty mark over top of lip with dark brown eyebrow pencil.

12.
Dust on a little peach blusher and blend so that the effect is subtle.

For a successful look, aim to create an illusion of similarity, rather than trying to draw a mask of Madonna's face onto your own. It is important to separate Madonna's stage look from her day look.

...&DAY

4.
Using a short bristled brush and matt, dark brown eyeshadow, brush shadow up and through eyebrows.

Madonna has thick brows towards the centre, narrowing up and out in an arched fashion; start off gently and stop and check result as you go. Brush brows through to blend the colour.

1.
Choose a light foundation that matches your own, natural skin tone; avoiding brands that are too pink in colour. Tip a little foundation onto the back of your hand and apply to the face with a cosmetic sponge, starting in the centre and sweeping outwards. Aim to create an invisible coverage, through to the jawline and hairline. Blend base over eyelids up to the brows and under the eye area.

2.
Hide any blemishes with a concealer that is slightly lighter than the base. If needed, add a little moisturiser to a dry concealer, so that it blends easily. Pat with fingertip. Use concealer under eye area, only where the line of shadow appears, and pat with fingertip.

3.
Apply a loose, translucent powder with a powder puff, with a firm pressing-and-rolling action. Use a small flat brush to powder around nose creases and over entire eye area. Brush off excess with a large brush in downward strokes.

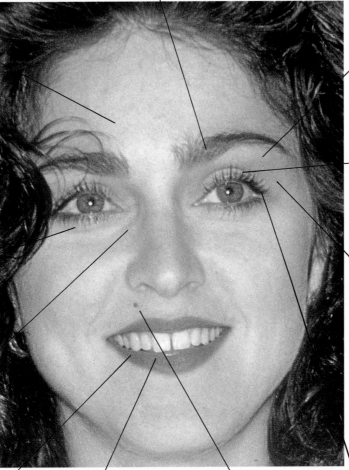

5.
Using an almost invisible, neutral matt eye colour (a face shader is ideal) brush over entire eye area, up to the brow.

6.
Using a matt, darkish brown or grey eyeshadow, sweep a line of colour into the socket line (the point at which the eyelid folds back into the eye socket). Bring the same colour across the outside of the eyelid and line next to upper lashes. Blend away.

7.
Using a matt, dark brown or black eyeshadow, with upwards and outwards strokes, blend a little shadow over the outer corner of the eye, and into the socket line. Sweep a little shadow under lower lashes, blend and soften. Use eyeshadow with a little water as eyeliner, and apply with a fine-tipped brush. Gently holding the brow-bone area enables you to apply eyeline really close to upper lashes. Lift line at outer edge to create wide-eyed look.

8.
Apply one coat of mascara to emphasise lashes, taking care not to clog them. Pay particular attention to outer lashes.

9.
Coat lips lightly with foundatioin and line with a pencil that is the same shade as your lipstick; just lining the centre-bottom lip and top arch will do.

10.
Using a good lipbrush, fill in lips with a matt, earthy, brownish-red or true-red lipstick. Take your time and get a perfect shape. Take lipstick over to the edge of the lipline to avoid a hard, pencilled outline. For a good, full shape, keep the bow rounded rather than pointed.

12.
Using a dark brown eyebrow pencil, gently dot on the famous beauty mark, just above the lips.

11.
Blot lips and dust over a small amount of loose powder. Apply another coat of lipstick.

'Marlene Dietrich is still sexy… I think she's maintained a sexual allure.'

to drink from it. Flirting with lesbianism, Madonna sits at a table with her arms around a girl she is about to kiss. Dressed as a butch mistress in a suit with her hair slicked back, Madonna is surrounded by 'transvestite supplicants' – men wearing feminine underwear, stockings and suspenders. Dressed as a pin-up girl in nothing but heels, seamed stockings and a garter belt, Madonna lays on top of a piano with an American flag wrapped around her, grinning and saluting. Throughout, her makeup reflects the thirties with thinly pencilled eyebrows, angular lips and dark, smudgy panda eyes.

Another set of photographs taken by Steven Meisel around the same time showed Madonna sitting cross-legged in fishnet tights – with no knickers underneath – and a bra; smiling, leering and finally gasping open-mouthed at a man who unzips his jeans and displays his wares to her.

With Madonna's 33rd birthday almost upon her, interviewer Carrie Fisher couldn't resist asking Madonna how long she intended using sex as such a vital element of her image. "In terms of your career," she probed, "won't you have to stop being as sexual at a certain point before it becomes weird?"

"Marlene Dietrich is still sexy," replied Madonna. "I think she's maintained a sexual allure. You just do it in a different way. I'm absolutely not afraid of whether I'll find work or not in ten years. What is going to be tougher for me is just the emotional side of being older." Madonna pointed out that she was more obsessed with death than eternal youth. "When I turned 30, which was the age my mother was when she died of breast cancer, I just flipped out because I kept thinking I'm now outliving my mother. I thought

something horrible was going to happen to me. Like, this is it, my time is up." Madonna fears death as the ultimate unknown. "I don't want to go to the dark beyond. I want to stay where I know where everything is."

In July, the controversial *In Bed With Madonna* film opened in England; a candid, fly-on-the-wall popumentary that aimed to demystify the razzle-dazzle of her super-stardom and present a more personal side of an icon. Film-maker Alek Keshishian spent every waking moment with Madonna on her Blonde Ambition tour in order to expose her body and soul, and bring to light some of the warmth and vulnerability that lay tucked away inside Madonna's sex-bomb (and some would say super-bitch) persona.

In the golden days of Hollywood, it was the duty of every celebrity to maintain a decent air of arms-length mystery – and the duty of the press to keep a respectable distance. When Madonna first became famous and the paparazzi started shadowing her every move, she mourned the passing of such protective standards. "I feel vulnerable. The press love to make you their darling but they only want you to go so far and then they take pleasure in ripping you to shreds."

Now, in an act of total surrender, Madonna had thrown the doors right open and declared herself public property. "I can't take a shit without reading about it. Everybody seems to know what I'm doing in life anyway, so I might as well not be ashamed or afraid to approach it in my artwork." Suddenly she seemed willing to explode the myth that she has spent so much time and care creating.

When interviewed in Cannes by Terry Wogan for his BBC show, Madonna told him how wor-

The Nineties Gypsy. *Evoke the romantic and passionate spirit of Frida Kahlo's Mexico (Madonna's favourite artist) with generous flounces and flamenco frills, lace, flamboyant prints and fedora hats. Team tiered or embroidered skirts with plunging necklines, off-the-shoulder blouses, and bold jewellery. For Madonna's gypsy-cum-rumba style, wear a tie-blouse with skintight trousers.*

Above: Madonna shows off her spectacular Marilyn Monroe jacket.

Petticoat Power. *Thanks to Madonna, sensuous lingerie came out of the closet in the 1991 fashion shows, as couture collections featured luxurious satin slips worn as sassy dresses with long evening gloves, and pretty lace petticoats worn as skirts with bustiers.*

Facing page: **Hours and hours spent in the gymnasium enable Madonna to perfect the physical contortions that play such a vital role in her stage shows.**

ried her manager Freddy DeMann had been by the project because he came from the old school of thought... "And that is that you have to have mystique about you all the time – people won't be interested if they know what you look like without your make-up on. Or when you're upset or when you're feeling tired you have to cloak yourself in this Garbo-esque aura of mystery or you will lose your appeal to people. But I don't agree with that and I don't think it's possible to reveal yourself completely."

The *New Musical Express* declared Madonna "A star for the voyeuristic age, an age when wars start on television and confession is only good for the soul if it's picked up by the wires."

An American entertainment magazine called *US* welcomed the film as a chance to get to know Madonna better. "During her recent cone-bra, geisha-android period, Madonna seemed well on her way to becoming a dehumanized Hollywood monster – one of those Terminator-type celebrities who can't be touched. But Madonna has made a career out of redefining her image. And the nicest thing about this film is that she's human again – or, at least, she's pretending to be. With Madonna, you never know for sure."

And at the end of the day Madonna's manager had to admit, "It works. The make up is off and all the gloves are off, and it's the *real* real."

While ex-beau Warren Beatty (a renowned privacy freak) reproached Madonna for... "The insanity of doing this all on a documentary" and fired his famous comment: "She doesn't want to live off camera, much less talk... what point is there existing?", Keshishian admired her guts for allowing unflattering shots of herself to remain in the final edit. "There wasn't a single frame of the

250 hours I shot that Madonna told me I couldn't use because she looked bad," he remarked. "At the very least you'd think she would have said, 'I don't look good in that shot... I look ugly', or something. Never. She never said it."

Far from exploding her own myth, Madonna's honesty had made her even more of a heroine. "Madonna is an antidote to most of the tripe we are offered," enthused Peter McKay of the *Evening Standard*. "She is demystifying show business... in the post-Madonna era, entertainers won't need to come on as shining pillars of virtue offstage. The longer she survives, the more difficult it becomes for any rivals to succeed with the schmaltzy old 'you lovely people' approach to audience seduction."

Critic Derek Malcolm agreed. "This wide-eyed truthfulness works in her favour. She thrives on surprise, doing what the rest of them up there in the pantheon of stardom wouldn't do. She's a very shrewd person, and this is a very shrewd film."

"In an odd sort of way this movie makes her an even greater myth," said Keshishian. "It's like you open a door to a house and you see one room, but realise there are so many other rooms you have no idea about."

"People will say, 'She knows the camera is on, she's just acting'," Madonna sighs resignedly, "But even if I am acting there's a truth in my acting... I wanted people to see that my life isn't so easy. While you get to know me to a certain degree... you could watch it and say, 'I still don't know Madonna', and good. Because you will never know the real me. Ever."

"Whether it's real or whether it's film is only important for her to know," smiles an enlightened

Freddie DeMann. "The fact that she keeps you guessing... well, she's already succeeded."

Madonna has complained that... "A lot of writers try to portray me as petulant, demanding, confrontational and overbearing. That's such a waste of time, and so tiresome, and it's not all there is to me. Nobody's one way." But however well anyone may think they know Madonna, she is a constant source of surprise and wonder when encountered in the flesh. Then, journalists never fail to fall under her spell; nor are they ever lost for words to describe their enchantment. This petite and pale media star makes them feel as if they have basked in the presence of ethereal royalty.

"Hair down, heels spiked, she radiates retro-glamour – a gossamer goddess in billowy black lounge wear with matching brassiere ... even her bearing seems a tad regal," gushed a *Rolling Stone* writer.

Vanity Fair also noted Madonna's regal air, saying that she moved like... "an indolent, trampy goddess." In a later issue, journalist Kevin Sessums went even further: "There is no trace of the indolence left, and only a bit of the trampiness. The regalness, however, has matured into a bearing so secure that she seems to be trailing an invisible train in her wake... she wears no make up except for the bit beneath her she-devil mole, below which resides the reddest lips allowed in town. She is the perfect femme fatale... bold, bullshitless, belligerently beautiful."

A *Daily Express* journalist who caught a glimpse of Madonna out jogging on her last tour remarked, "She looks like a Dresden doll. Tiny frame, transparent pale skin, luminous blue eyes, topped with a baseball cap to shade her white face from the sun."

Adrian Deevoy was charmed when sent to her Hollywood home on behalf of *Q* magazine. "Her entrance is just nonchalant enough not to appear choreographed. She sweeps into the room and regally presents her hand, high enough to either kiss or shake, all the while fixing you with a smiling, soul-scrutinising stare. Her eyes are an unimaginable blue. Displaying the self-conscious grace of a small girl attempting to keep her mother's shoes on, she moves slowly and deliberately... she looks sickeningly healthy and radiates fitness. She is smaller than you'd expect, even when you were expecting her to be small. She is, in the flesh, uncommonly beautiful."

The Guardian's highly respected critic, Derek Malcolm, was also bewitched when he was sent, against his will, to interview Madonna in Cannes. After reportedly snorting, "I don't want to interview that bloody awful woman!", there was an immediate softening the moment he came face to face with her. "Thinking is difficult when faced with this attractive but not conventionally beautiful woman who answers questions very directly and, if they are stupid, doesn't hesitate to say so," he confessed. "She does appear – and it's the only

The Bikini. Conceived by Louis Reard in 1946, the bikini was denounced by the Catholic Church and immortalised by Marilyn Monroe. Today's stretch Lycra two-pieces can be worn as Madonna-style bustier tops and hot pants. Fifties-inspired swimsuits with moulded cups, decorated with sequins or tassels, can be worn as glamorous tops under denim shorts or skirts.

"The Nineties woman chooses her image. This time around the joke is on the men… Madonna is the one manning the controls. She's powerful and free to portray her sexuality how SHE chooses."
Observer Magazine, June 1991.

"I suppose Madonna's major contribution to fashion has been the tin tit, but she's the most unseductive thing that's ever had a pair of boobs."
Sir Hardy Amis.

Following pages: Gaultier's pointed bras, originally seen in the Forties, were the essential element of Madonna's on stage look during the 'Who's That Girl' tour which wound its way around the world in 1987.

word that springs readily to mind, however feeble – nicer than one would expect from so immensely ambitious and sharp a generator of instant publicity... it may have been a carefully manufactured showbiz personality, but it now fits her like a glove and it was undoubtedly manufactured by herself. You don't get the sense that she's saying what she ought to say – like the stars of the Hollywood that doesn't really comprehend what she is about at all." Malcolm had started to comprehend – he even regretted not turning up with some flowers for her.

The Sunday Times sent Robert Sandall to interview Madonna in Cannes. He was taken aback by her piercing gaze. "You noticed it immediately in her wide, tired eyes. You couldn't help it, because the first surprise – more disconcerting than her sudden and virtually unannounced arrival in the room, more arresting than the newly styled dark brown straight hair or the plunging neckline of her black trouser suit – was Madonna's penetrating stare. Icons are for looking at. But the most famous female one since Marilyn Monroe discouraged any casual gawping by, at all times, outgazing her interviewer. Madonna never spoke without first establishing unblinkingly direct eye contact."

Madonna looks away, however, when she's out walking the streets, as *Vanity Fair* journalist Lynn Hirschberg discovered when accompanying her one evening. "Tonight she is dressed like a street urchin – a schoolboy's cap covers her hair completely and she wears no make-up. Madonna stares at the ground when she walks, careful not to make eye contact with passers-by. The strategy works, even though the streets are relatively crowded, Madonna walks home without causing a commotion."

Film maker Alek Keshishian adds, "When Madonna puts on her cap and overcoat she looks like a twelve-year-old boy, straight from the cast of *Oliver*. She wore that one day in Los Angeles when we went to a club, and when we left, the valet guy goes, 'Are you leaving so soon? I hear Madonna's in there.' And he was looking right at her when he said it!"

The only media type who did not appear overjoyed at having been granted an audience with Madonna was chat show host Terry Wogan, who interviewed her with much fanfare for what was the 1000th edition of his early evening BBC show. For once – and probably unwisely – Wogan left the cosy confines of his Shepherds Bush studio and travelled to Cannes to meet his 'guest' (Wogan, of course, was really Madonna's 'guest') but it was a predictable mismatch: the ever cheerful but frequently naïve and certainly unhip Irish veteran and the most fashion conscious and liberated female sex symbol of the past decade. The age and attitude gaps were all too clear to see: Madonna showed up in a low-cut emerald satin mini-dress worn over leggings, her dark hair centre-parted and flicked up at the sides;

Above: **Like all instantly recognisable celebrities, Madonna avoids eye contact with strangers when out on the streets.**

Facing Page: **Barry Humphries' Edna Everage creation might have inspired this curious costume Madonna wore during one section of the 'Who's That Girl' show.**

"She's not a particularly good looking girl...I've talked to people who, in the fullness of time will be seen to be greater stars, but she's the one who talks, believes and lives it."
Terry Wogan, 1990.

The face that launched a thousand covers… 'Everywhere you look there is either Madonna herself or a kind of echo of her'.

Graffiti artist _Keith Haring_ customised a pair of denim cut-offs for Madonna; make your own with studs, sequins and marker pens. Wear over a black Lycra catsuit with a denim jacket and cap.

in contrast, Wogan looked like a middle-aged English tourist on a golfing holiday, even down to finding the heat discomforting. While acknowledging that Madonna was: "The biggest thing to hit the Cannes Film Festival in years... even the legendary Bardot never got the French this worked up," Wogan felt shunned by her apparent disinterest in him when they were introduced.

"She's small, not exactly pretty, wary. She gives off no warmth, she doesn't smile a lot... She seems embattled, cornered, caged by a circus of her own creating. She's defensive, tough, articulate and honest. You can see that she's impatient and quick to anger." Wogan had found her to be an intimidating and unreachable star. On his show, he even confessed to Madonna that he was afraid of her.

In the beginning, _Rolling Stone_ put Madonna's success down to the fact that she was not some unattainable icon – but a real person like her fans. These days Madonna wannabes do have a lot more to live up to: high-fashion, total fitness, unswerving dedication, and an all-consuming ambition.

An article on 'The Immaculate Conceptions' by Michael Musto in _US_ magazine examined the new breed of wannabes. "The Madonna wannabe phenomenon may have peaked a few years ago – it was a lot easier for teenage girls to mimic the thrift shop lace-and-crucifix look than to wear Bob Mackie gowns - but Madonna's impact as a role model is stronger than ever. The message her success has imparted to young people everywhere is: It doesn't matter if you're not the most talented actress or singer in the world, or the most naturally beautiful person. If you work hard enough and package yourself properly you can will yourself to stardom."

In a feature for the _Evening Standard_, Nigella Lawson agreed that Madonna was "The Billy Liar who made it, the glorious product of her own grandiose imagination." She went on to make the point that... "It is notable that the people Madonna draws are women. She is of little interest to men, straight men, that is. Her erotic pull is for women. Women love watching her and she throws a line out to them... she appeals to the narcissist and exhibitionist in us all."

A July issue of the London guide _Time Out_ dedicated six of its pages to features that examined 'The Cloning of Madonna'. Writer Julie Burchill scrutinised the starlet 'apostles' who were aspiring to fill Madonna's shoes: "Just as Garbo made a physical difference to many actresses of the thirties, Cher, Kylie, Estefan, even the wretched Bans (Bananarama), all of them have taken to putting on their underwear over their outerwear. When Annie Lennox appears in a brassière, she makes it look like the desperate flash of a disturbed person; Madonna makes it look like fun. Kylie with a whip looks like a little girl at a fancy dress party; Madonna makes it look dirty." Burchill dismissed pop's famous wan-

nabes by pronouncing judgement: "Madonna's enjoyment and confidence are not only unshakeable; they are unfakeable."

Another _Time Out_ spread featured a 'Clone Rangers' chart that measured the Madonna potential of 'this year's models'. Candidates included Betty Boo, Kylie Minogue, Patsy Kensit, Prince, Marilyn Monroe, Wendy James, Cyndi Lauper and (cheekily) The Virgin Mary. Categories included Over-underwear, Fitness Freak, Sexually Outrageous, Ego, Religion, Hairhopping, Acting Ability and Swearing.

And here are the results of the pretender contenders – Monroe was recognised as the original Madonna prototype; Cyndi Lauper as a slightly earlier model; and Prince as the male Madonna. Kylie was exposed as a total fraud because 'a shoddy conversion job cannot turn a bubble-gum dispenser into a sex machine.' And The Virgin Mary scored high in the hair-hopping category because... "she changes her hair in every portrait, though the halo remains the same". _Time Out_ declared that... "In the end there's only one Madonna. She may have shared the '80s with Michael Jackson and Prince... but so far in the '90s there's no one to touch her for star appeal and stubborn staying power. A miracle of engineering."

The Madonna for the nineties has become the first 'ALL ACCESS' icon. Seated on her unshakeable and unpredictable throne, she regally offers her hand to the world at her feet, desperately longing for approval, yet equally relishing disapproval. "She seems like an absolute presence in culture," said American cultural historian Greil Marcus, when interviewed for the BBC _Omnibus_ documentary. "Everywhere you look there is either Madonna herself or a kind of echo of her." The Madonna 'myth' lives on because she will always be a 'Who's That Girl?' phenomenon.

"What is this thing called Madonna?" writer Julie Burchill once asked. "This – not any record or film – is her ultimate triumph. That seven years later we are still asking."

When Madonna started out she said that she wanted to stand for "Positive life-messages... dreams and magic and things that are happy." Kristine McKenna of the _Los Angeles Times_ believes that Madonna has achieved this aim. "She's the epitome of everything that's considered important now in popular culture. Society needs goddess and god figures... people project all kinds of things on to her but she's really not known in a way, so she's a kind of a repository for dreams for people."

"What you have to understand with Madonna," says her manager Freddie DeMann, "is that she has substance. People forget that. Since she reinvents herself all the time and does these provocative things, people tend to concentrate on her image of the moment. But there is substance there. If you only resort to provocation, you don't last long."

Madonna plucks from the past, the present and the future for inspiration and ideas, always keeping her eyes open. Anything that takes her fancy can be moulded to suit her purposes.

Left: **The image of Madonna's namesake came into focus during the Blond Ambition tour when Madonna adopted the Confessional position during 'Like A Prayer'.**

Far left: **Keith Haring was a brilliant New York artist, a former graffitist. He designed Madonna's early stage outfits, including the ultra colourful costume she wore for most of the 'Like A Virgin' shows. She was devastated when Haring died of AIDS in 1990, and her subsequent concern for AIDS charities reflects their close relationship.**

(NY106)NEW YORK, Oct.24—VICTORY—Alberto Salazar of the United States raises three fingers to signify three consecutive New York City Marathon victories Sunday, as he crosses the finish line first in the 42.2 Km. race in 2:09:29.(AP Laserphoto)(msl 1418stf/suzanne vlamis)1982

Left: **The modern American is preoccupied by fitness, as shown by the New York Marathon. Madonna is no exception. To be upwardly mobile in America is to visit the gym regularly...and few Americans are more upwardly mobile, or fit, than Madonna.**

Far left: **Marlon Brando and James Dean gave their seal of approval to the leather jacket in the Fifties. It became one of the few constants in fashion. Classic black or brightly coloured, it's a basic to Madonna's style.**

INFLUENCES & HEROES/PART 3

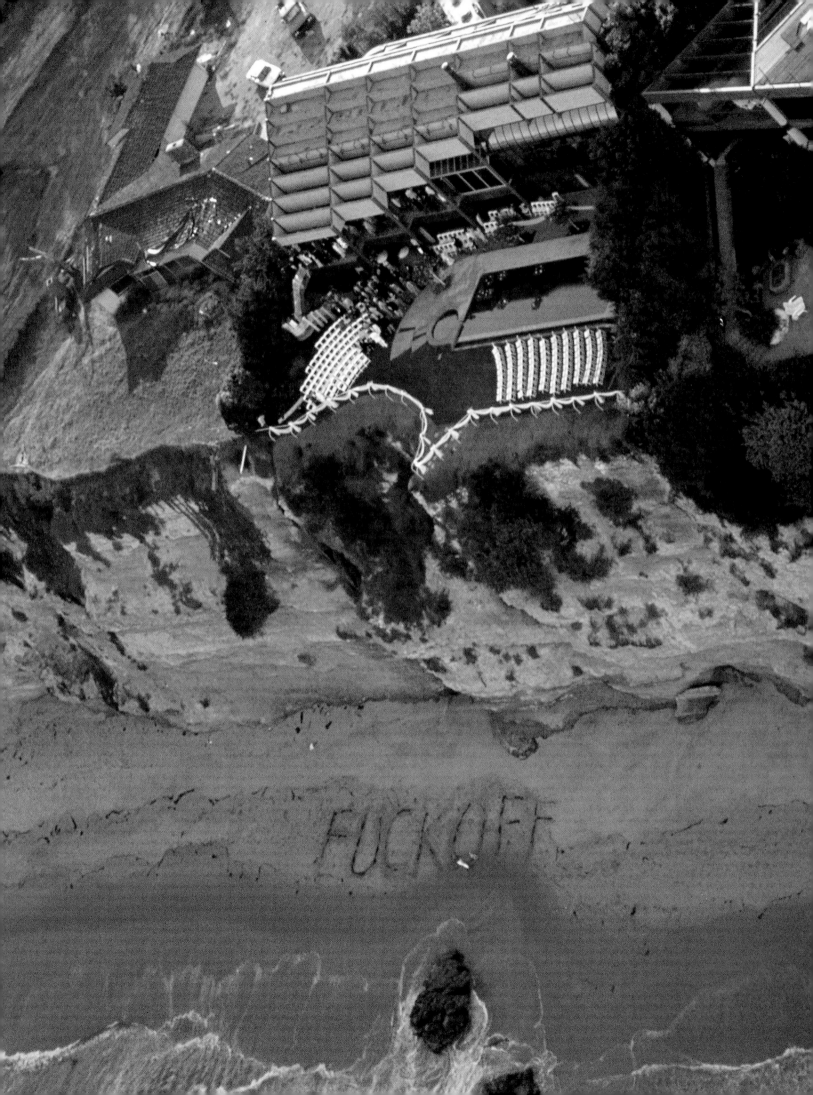

SEX & RELIGION

Madonna Louise Veronica Ciccone was born on August 16, 1958, and named after her Italian/American mother, an angelic woman who died when Madonna was only six-and-a-half-years-old. Madonna is her real name and not, as might reasonably be assumed, a stage name dreamt up by some imaginative Hollywood publicity agent with a taste for quasi-religious icons. Nevertheless, it is a rare and controversial name which conjures up powerful images of innocence, mystery, purity and strength, but it also carries with it an inherent burden – an obligation to become someone "extra specially supercharged", as Madonna herself once put it.

Whether Madonna's mother intentionally blessed her with this name because she knew it would give her something to live up to, Madonna will never know for sure, but she has one theory: "It's very rare for an Italian Catholic mother to name her daughter after her, so I think in a way that maybe it was meant to happen that she died when I was so young."

Madonna's name didn't make her the brunt of any childish jokes at school because she had a Catholic education. "I didn't get made fun of... and I never remember feeling tormented for my name." But in Italy, where the name is commonly taken in vain as a curse, "... everyone tells me that it's sacrilegious."

When she was growing up in car factory towns in and around Detroit, Madonna felt at one with her body, and claims to have been in touch with her sensuality since the tender age of five. "I've been provoking people since I was a little girl. I was very interested in being alluring... I remember liking my body and not feeling inhibited. Maybe it comes from having older brothers and sisters and sharing the bathroom."

Sexually aroused at the age of 7, Madonna satisfied some of her curiosity by experimenting with girlfriends. "I think that's really normal... you get really curious and there's your girlfriend, she's spending the night, and it happens."

Religion, too, was experienced in a passionate and adolescent way. Madonna thought the devil lived in the basement of her home – and tried to grab her ankles every time she ran upstairs. "I did a lot of bad things and I didn't feel guilty about it because I knew I could go to confession at the end of the week and all would be forgiven."

She had her first crush on Jesus Christ. "He was like a movie star, my favourite idol of all... I chose Veronica as my confirmation name because she wiped the face of Jesus." And she thought nuns were... "superhuman, beautiful, fantastic people, really elegant. They wore those long gowns, they seemed to glide on the floor. Everyone said that they were married to Jesus." Madonna even thought that crucifixes were erotic... "because there's a naked man on them."

Madonna was 10 years old when her step-mother told her about the facts of life for the first time. Her step-daughter was doing the washing up at the time and she was utterly horrified at what

"Passion and sexuality and religion all bleed into each other for me. I think that you can be a very sexual person and also a very religious and spiritual person... making love can be a spiritual experience."

Facing page: The aerial view of Madonna's wedding in Malibu to Sean Penn on August 16, 1985. Before the ceremony guests took the opportunity to write a forthright message in the sand to the hovering paparazzi.

'Oh my God! What if my father sees this?'

she heard. "Every time she said the word 'penis' I'd turn the water on really hard so it would drown out what she said... I can barely relate to a dick now, I couldn't at all then... I was shocked when I saw my first one. I thought it was really gross."

Madonna decided that she would aspire to become either a superstar or a nun, innocently believing both to be sexy and above-average people. "Then the nuns announced to me that a girl who wanted to be a nun was very modest and not interested in boys. After that my role model was my ballet teacher."

When Madonna met Christopher Flynn, her whole world changed. "It wasn't just because studying dance with him gave me a focus and took me out of what I considered to be a very humdrum existence... he also took me out to my first gay discotheque and I saw a different side of life than anything I've ever seen before."

Madonna has said that she lost her virginity at the age of 14 to someone she loved, and that her father never knew. "My parents were virgins when they got married... I think my father realised I was having sex once I married Sean. Before then I don't think he did." Madonna's father haunts her conscience whenever she does anything she knows he'd find shocking. Like the time she posed naked in Vanity Fair and suddenly thought, "Oh my God, what if my father sees this? He'll see me without a shirt on... it's not that I'm frightened of being scolded, I'm past all that, but I just don't want him to be hurt."

Today Madonna describes herself as a fallen Catholic, but the most extraordinary irony is that she has become something of a religion herself; a living, breathing icon, prepared to expose the world for its shortcomings. "I sometimes think I was born to live up to my name," Madonna muses. "How could I be anything else but what I am, having been named Madonna? I would either have ended up a nun or this."

Fearlessly, she points an accusing finger at America for wallowing in the kind of moral ignorance that allows so much prejudice to thrive. "In America we've still got this stupid residue of false values... I break the rules. So I'm some kind of monster. If they are shocked by me, they can go to hell." She roars with disapproval at the Catholic Church for its repressive dogma, sexist attitude and tortuous cycle of sin, guilt and punishment. "The church has filled so many people with a lot of terrible fears... if I do any good at all, it's to loosen things up."

In a telling moment from her documentary film, Madonna admits, "I know that I'm not the best singer and I'm not the best dancer, but I'm not interested in that. I'm interested in pushing people's buttons." Madonna is like the mythological Pandora, opening a box that contains the ills and taboos of mankind and forcing everyone to face them. "If you're afraid of me then you're afraid of what I make you feel."

She has made it her mission to use her power as a role model to challenge traditional beliefs, and even to prove that sex and spirituality can coexist. "I know the ignorance people prefer to live in – because it's easier for them. I'm just trying to pull their Band Aids off."

When Terry Wogan asked Madonna if she thought she was a suitable role model for her young fans she replied, "I think I stand for freedom of expression, for being honest, for saying what I believe in, for going after your dreams... yes, I think I am a good role model."

Blessed are the persecuted, for they have Madonna as their spokesperson. "It excites me to be a political person. I'm incensed by the prejudices of the world... I'm willing to sacrifice my private life if it will change people's points of view about life and the phobias they have."

When Madonna uses her celebrity as a platform to re-educate people she aims where it hurts; right in the crotch of the matter. This is best reflected in her campaign against intolerance towards homosexuals and support for AIDS research and education. "I am constantly trying to challenge the accepted ways of behaving sexually. Straight men need to be emasculated. I'm sorry. They all need to be slapped around. Women have been kept down for too long. Every straight guy should have a man's tongue in his mouth at least once."

There is no time for any gentle awakening on Madonna's furious crusade. She denies being addicted to scandal and refuses to acknowledge any shame, but because she so often chooses to throw down the gauntlet on controversial topics, her positive life-messages can get lost in the ensuing commotion. Her directness inevitably causes those within earshot to react on two entirely different levels – with love and hate. Madonna's character as Breathless Mahoney in *Dick Tracy* couldn't have put it better when she says: "You don't know if you want to hit me or kiss me, I get a lot of that."

In *Rolling Stone*, Carrie Fisher accused Madonna of being an unscrupulous focus puller. "You enjoy being controversial. That used to mean talking about things that were never talked about. Now it seems controversy is just a diluted form of pornography or obscenity." While American columnist Liz Smith empathised: "Madonna's humanism may not be yours – too vulgarly expressed; too provocatively presented, or just too much... but behind the shock and her unabashed satisfaction with her own success is a message of tolerance and humanism."

Christopher Ciccone denies that his sister works out any deliberate strategies to gain all this attention. "It's just who she is and what she does. And there is definitely a cost." When *Sky* magazine put it to Madonna that... "Most women get punished for being sexual in public, but you get rewarded." She replied, "But I've been punished too... it's much more acceptable for men in the music industry to act in an overtly sexual way...

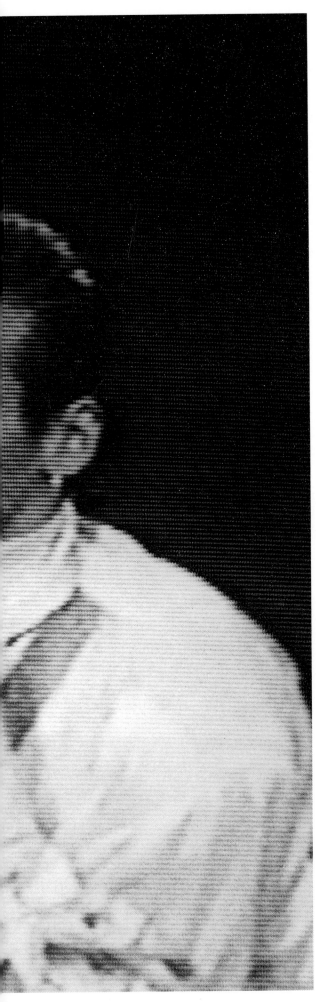

instead of concentrating on my music and my message, people get bogged down in my sexuality... but I don't go around complaining that I'm getting the shaft. Really it's made me work harder."

At the top of Madonna's taboo list is Catholicism, a difficult habit to shake by all accounts. "Once you're a Catholic you're always a Catholic – in terms of your feelings of guilt and remorse – traditionally you are a sinner. I mean the idea is that when Adam and Eve ate from the apple, or had sex, from that day on they were considered sinners, and all human beings are considered sinners. So you're always striving to be good... I'm often wracked with guilt when I needn't be... and it's hard for me to enjoy the things which I don't think I deserve."

Madonna has been willing to acknowledge the positive side of her religion. "Catholicism gives you an inner strength. I'm self-disciplined because I went to Catholic school and my father was very strict... I wouldn't have turned out the way I did if I didn't have all those old-fashioned values to rebel against." But much of Madonna's work revolves around dealing with ingrained religious hang-ups and exorcising what she calls her 'demons'.

She has said that... "My Catholic upbringing is probably the foundation of everything I do right now." But while disapproving of organised religion, Madonna still believes in God. "The thing is that I'm a true believer, but a sceptic as far as the church is concerned... I think God is in everything... I don't like to have to visit God in a specific area. I like him to be everywhere. Part of my air."

She still prays, constantly. "I don't think guilt or shame are synonymous with prayer... If something's really horrible and I say enough prayers it will get better... God seems to be there whenever things are really horrible. I do try to remind myself – I know this sounds corny – to be thankful for things when they're good, to be conscious of God." A communal prayer circle was held immediately before every show on the Blond Ambition tour, an essential ritual that Madonna sees as both unifying and strengthening. "It's a way to get people focused and together." At the end of each prayer session Madonna would rouse her dancers to battle with the cry: "Amen, everyone have a great show."

Church is a place Madonna still visits occasionally, purely to soak up the atmosphere. "I love the rituals, particularly of Catholicism, and the architecture of grand, beautiful churches and the mysteriousness of it all... and the incense and the classic organ music. It's a beautiful ritual but often the messages are not so beautiful."

Madonna has said that she started wearing rosaries as necklaces because, for her, they represented suffering. "I was exercising the extremes my Catholic upbringing dwelt on. Putting them up on the wall and throwing darts at them."

"*Madonna repeatedly shows an ability to re-invent herself with a rapidity that manages to retain even the short attention span of a generation of adolescents, who do little but endlessly watch pop videos on cable television. From blonde to brunette and back to blonde, from virgin to whore and all things in between... It is hardly a healthy role model Madonna presents to the so-called teenage girl 'wannabes', to whom she is so vacantly nihilistic a symbol of our age. But such is Madonna's rainbow of public personas, her mania for hard work and her ruthless determination to succeed that she could end up having the last laugh on all of us.*"
Sunday Observer, July 1990.

As the most successful female singer in the history of pop music, Madonna has influenced virtually every rival, whether it be in the music they record, the way they present it or the clothes they wear. Still, this is nothing new…

A post-Madonna parade of exposed bras, bare navels, dangling crucifixes, layered jewellery and Monroesque make-up, all of it inspired by Madonna…
Clockwise from top left: **Gloria Estefan, Wendy James, Prince, Annie Lennox, Patsy Kensit, Bananarama and Cher.**

Above: **Great minds think alike: Cyndi Lauper in 1985 displayed the look she established in parallel to Madonna, but never capitalised on it in the manner that Madonna did.**

Facing page: **Many performers have borrowed ideas from Madonna, some more flagrantly than others. Mostly it's a case of exposed underwear. Where Madonna treads down the path of explicitness, others follow, none more blatantly than Kylie Minogue. Her 1991 concerts at Wembley featured the 'Neighbours' star in fishnets and black underwear that might have been filched from Madonna's closet. Kylie's transformation from girl-next-door to half-dressed siren was a desperate attempt to update her image. It failed.**

THE COPYCATS

As for crucifixes: "They're something left over from my childhood, like a security blanket."

Carl Arrington of *People* magazine believes that Madonna... "has seized back the crucifix for the masses... suddenly the crucifix as a fashion icon is something that caught people's imaginations, partly because they want something to believe in other than a Coca Cola logo."

Madonna's smear campaign against Catholicism for its inability to provide any soothing solutions in these troubled times has reached into the very sacred heart of the Vatican itself. Like some fallen, blaspheming angel with tired wings and a tarnished halo, dull with disillusionment, Madonna prods away at the smug underbelly of Catholicism with her barbed comments and loaded lyrics. "I do think someone is protecting me. I don't know if it's an angel. It could be the devil." Determined to rock the very foundations of the Vatican, Madonna keeps on hurling profanities in their face.

"My ultimate goal is to stand next to God," Madonna announced to *The Face* magazine back in 1985, while at the same time confessing that she lost her virginity as a career move. Her famous quote about growing up with two extreme images of women – the virgin and the whore – perhaps explains why sex and religion have become such inevitable and inextricable bedfellows in Madonna's work.

"My problem with the Catholic Church is that they have always separated sexuality and spirituality... it's just a way of controlling people. That's why they freak out when they see me dressed in a corset with a crucifix hanging around my neck." In one of her most controversial interviews, with American gay magazine *Advocate*, Madonna went on to say: "Your sexual life is supposed to be dead if you're a good Catholic. It's human nature to be sexual, so why would God want you to deny your human nature? Mary Magdalene was considered a fallen woman because she slept with men, but Jesus said it was okay. I think they probably got it on, Jesus and Mary Magdalene."

In the gospel according to Madonna, sex makes the world go round, but in ways that go beyond trousers and crude vulgarity. "Sex is the reason for everything. That's why I'm here, because my parents had sex... People's sexuality and the way they relate to the world is very important... The more you pay attention to your sexual identity, the more you realise that just about everything in the world is centred around sexual attraction and sexual power."

Man had always been the traditional sexual aggressor, until Madonna came along. "I like the idea of men being the objects of desire, the sirens that entrap women, instead of the other way around." This twisting of sexual stereotypes gives us a glimpse of a matriarchal world where femininity equals power, where women have control, and where a man's strength lies in his

sensitivity. "It's scary for men that women would have that power, and it's scary for women to have that power and be sexy at the same time." If you feel uncomfortable with Madonna's role reversing portrayal of men and women, then good, because she intends to be a sexual threat and to inspire arguments about sexual values.

Madonna has said that she has both a hostility towards men "which rears its ugly head often in my work" and a need to explore her masculine side. "I think like a guy, but I'm feminine. So I relate to feminine men." She is fascinated by gay culture and has a theory that all human beings are innately bisexual. She enjoyed causing an uproar when she led the American public to believe that she was having an affair with her lesbian friend, comedienne Sandra Bernhard.

"I'd rather be male. When I was a little girl I was insanely jealous of my older brothers. They didn't have curfews, they could pee standing up, they could take their shirts off in the summer... they had so much more freedom... it would be great to be both sexes."

Madonna has said that she is closer to her gay brother Christopher Ciccone than anyone else in her family, and she surrounded herself with gay male dancers on her Blond Ambition tour. "Effeminate men intrigue me more than anything in the world. I see them as my alter egos... I feel their persecution, but also their sense of humour; and their willingness to deal with sexuality in an unconventional way is really interesting to me."

Madonna's favourite scene in the film *In Bed With Madonna* is the footage of two of her gay dancers engaged in a passionate kiss. "Hopefully people are going to see two men kissing and see that it's a beautiful thing... I love that people are going to watch that and go home and talk about it all night long. I live for things like that."

Madonna openly supports the lifestyle of gay people at a time when AIDS has reinforced the prejudices of many heterosexuals. She is pro life, pro equality and pro humanity. "That's not really the mood America's in right now. It's frightened of AIDS, it's turned everybody into these fifties monsters... it gives people a reason to vent their true feelings about homosexuality." Even the Catholic Church has turned its back. "I think it sucks the big one. I think it's disgusting. And it's unloving. It's not what God and Christianity are about."

Because she has known so many people who have died from AIDS, most notably her friend the gay New York artist Keith Haring, Madonna is determined to do anything she can to promote AIDS education, awareness and prevention. She preaches safe sex and the use of condoms to her young following. "Condoms are such a drag... they interrupt everything... they're not great but they make sense. They've saved my life." A fact sheet about AIDS was given away with copies of Madonna's *Like A Prayer* album. Defending the sexual content of some of her videos, Madonna

Above: Madonna lets her hair down at the AIDS Dance-A-Thon in Los Angeles, April 1991.

Facing page: As catwalk model during a celebrity fashion show for AIDS research, November 1986. Of all the charitable causes that Madonna has adopted, finding a cure for AIDS tops the list.

protested that she was not being hypocritical and promoting irresponsible promiscuity. "I'm saying I have a pussy and I'm dealing with my sexuality and you can deal with yours if you want to. You can have sex, but you have to practise safe sex. I think it's horrible that everyone thinks, Oh, my God! AIDS! Now we all have to sleep alone... use your imagination. Be creative."

Madonna has been happy to let the world think that her interest in gay culture has led to her own flirtations with lesbianism. "I think gay women would want to claim me as their own because I am a really strong woman. I am assertive in a way that a lot of gay women are, and I could be a really good mascot for them." Madonna's friendship with Sandra Bernhard when she was appearing in *Speed The Plow* and Sandra was doing a downtown show sparked off yet more fodder for the gossip columnists. "We were both stuck there for the summer so we just started hanging out and became really good friends."

Bernhard's openness about her lesbian affairs caused speculation about the nature of her relationship with Madonna. Adding fuel to the fire when they appeared on the David Letterman show together, Bernhard announced that she had

Madonna and her friend comedienne Sandra Bernhard parade matching outfits. Favoured costumes for their nights on the town in 1988.

slept with both Madonna and Sean Penn, while Madonna said they hung out together in Greenwich Village lesbian bars. Madonna enjoyed keeping people guessing about the real truth. "Whether I'm gay or not is irrelevant. Whether I slept with her or not is irrelevant. I'm perfectly willing to have people think that I did... and if it makes people feel safer to think that I didn't, then that's fine too."

So much moral outrage has been started by Madonna with a kiss. "Only great minds can be good kissers," she once boasted. "If you kiss well you're brilliant." In March 1989 Madonna kissed a black Jesus Christ in her video for 'Like A Prayer'. In November 1990 she kissed an androgynous model called Amanda Cazalet in her video for 'Justify My Love'. Each wave of controversy only served to heighten Madonna's profile – and her profits.

The 'Like A Prayer' video sent shivers up the spine of the Catholic and Christian world. Greil Marcus, the writer and American cultural historian, said it was... "as strong and upsetting a piece of public work that you are going to see anywhere". Madonna dances on a hill in front of half a dozen blazing crucifixes, kisses the feet of – and hints at having sex with – a black saint, who could be Jesus Christ himself. And then there was the outrageous ambiguity of the lyric: "I'm down on my knees. I want to take you there." Was Madonna saying her prayers or giving head?

Said Marcus, "She is threatening the taken-for-granted beliefs of how things ought to be for millions and millions of people." A storm of protest from religious pressure groups forced Pepsi Cola to bow to their fury and drop its multimillion dollar advertising campaign with Madonna for fear of a national boycott. Madonna adopted her usual "What's the big deal?" attitude and argued that the video was about racial harmony, morality and justice. "It dealt with a lot of taboos and I think the people who reacted negatively to it were afraid of their own feelings that they have about those issues."

John Baptiste Mondino shot the video for 'Justify My Love' in Paris. His idea was simply "to lock ourselves in a hotel for two days and one night without going out and just see what happens... It's very real – that's what's so shocking about it." A semi-naked Madonna and her then current boyfriend Tony Ward, writhe together on a bed and exchange kisses that were far from cinema kisses. But the shot that caused the most offence in this steamy scenario was of Madonna kissing model Amanda Cazalet while Ward sat on the edge of the bed, watching. According to Mondino, this was not part of some contrived storyboard. "It just happened that way... with AIDS, shouldn't we celebrate kissing as a beautiful thing."

"I am aroused by the idea of a woman making love to me while either another man or woman watches," said Madonna. Her portrayal of this

Facing Page: Madonna's erotic performance of 'Like A Virgin' during the 'Blond Ambition' tour was the most controversial aspect of the show, and brought condemnation from the Church for its erotic pseudo-masturbation sequence. Police threatened to arrest Madonna during the Canadian leg of the tour and there were problems in Italy where the Vatican took a dim view of her blatant use of sexuality.

"One month shy of her 32nd birthday Madonna cuts a hard, muscular figure, a superb if somewhat pneumatic advertisement for the weightlifting, jogging, fitness-conscious Eighties... the latest additions to her use of corsetry as an external fashion item were the conical D-cup monstrosities of designer Jean Paul Gaultier, not so much bras as gladiatorial accessories."
The Times, July 1990.

"Throughout history, female warriors have paraded their strength... the female form has been used to symbolise desirable qualities. From the mythical Britannia and the Statue of Liberty to the modern day 'Iron Lady', women have been used in allegory to portray strength, justice, truth and freedom."
Elle magazine, 1990.

fantasy led to an MTV ban, and there were even accusations that if you played the single backwards, Madonna had recorded a hidden message for Satan worshippers. "Why is it that people are willing to go to a movie and watch someone get blown to bits for no reason and nobody wants to see two girls kissing or two men snuggling?" asked an incensed Madonna. "I want people to deal with it. I want people to see it."

Public curiosity was aroused and Madonna's video became the biggest seller of its type in the United States. When she was later photographed kissing another girl for a *Rolling Stone* session, Carrie Fisher asked her if women kissed the same as men. "Sometimes, better," Madonna teased. "I've certainly had fantasies... but I'm not a lesbian."

At last – the rumour was squashed – and Madonna had to admit that... "I know I like to provoke, but this year has been like a train out of control."

On an American TV programme called Nightline, Madonna was called upon to justify the sexual content of her videos, and she in turn accused the American media of pretending that sex didn't exist. "The networks won't even play ads on TV that are about condoms, about birth control, about practising safe sex. We're pretending like we don't have a lot of teenagers that are having sex in the world, right now. Why are we subjecting ourselves to this kind of ignorance?"

She explained that she was against violence, humiliation and degradation on television... "and I don't think any of these issues are evident in my videos." She denied that there was any degradation invovled when she was naked and chained to a bed in the video for 'Express Yourself' because... "There wasn't a man who put the chain on me. I did it myself. I was chained to my desires... The sexuality in my videos is all consented to. No one's taking advantage of each other." She hoped her video for 'Justify My Love' provoked discussion between kids and their parents. "Let their parents explain to them that it is a sexual fantasy and that these things exist in life... it's not a pretty picture necessarily... but it's reality."

In a furious monologue to the camera Madonna answered her critics by concluding, "I'm in charge of my fantasies, I put myself in these situations with men, and everybody knows – in terms of my image with the public – I'm in charge of my career and my life."

For this reason Madonna thought it would be obvious that she was just having a little fun when she released the 'Hanky Panky' spanking song. It was written about her character in *Dick Tracy*, Breathless Mahoney, who likes getting slapped around by the gangsters she hangs out with. But when people thought Madonna was singing about her own kinky desire to play the victim, she decided to have a little more fun by playing up to their expectations.

"I admit I have this feeling that I'm a bad girl and I need to be punished," Madonna told one magazine. "I like dark brooding men with rough tempers. Italian men like to dominate and sometimes I like to cast myself in the submissive role," Madonna told another. Finally she admitted, "It's a joke. I despise being spanked. I absolutely detest it." Carrie Fisher admonished Madonna for her confusing sense of humour when she interviewed her for *Rolling Stone*. "If kids hear some of that stuff and think it's cute, it could be misinterpreted... you could be a little bit clearer about that, to my mind."

"I didn't mean it that way," she replied. "I think it was just my sick little sense of humour, or not-so-little sense of humour."

Madonna's most potent mixture of sexual and religious imagery was unleashed on her 1990 Blond Ambition tour, when the extreme and powerful presentations of her songs almost got her arrested in Canada and banned from Italy. Vatican propaganda resulted in low ticket sales and the cancellation of some shows. Blasphemy, swearing, violence and sex were the reasons for the outrage, but Madonna saw her show as a celebration of life... "a piece of theatre that provoked thought and took you on an emotional journey. I see happiness, I see sadness, I see sorrow, I see joy. I see religious passion and I see overt sexuality. I see all these different things and I was describing life, I wasn't saying you should live your life this way."

The real bête noire of Madonna's show was her bizarre interpretation of 'Like a Virgin' in which she lay upon a velvet bed, attended by two of her black male dancers, dressed as hermaphrodites in exaggeratedly pointed bras. They arouse her with kisses in intimate places until Madonna begins to explore her own body, simulating masturbation and reaching an earth-moving climax. "And then I hear the voice of God and the crucifix came down out of the ceiling and I was in church and I was now going to be punished, or go to confession and deal with the male authority figures – whether that's my father or a priest or the Pope or whatever – so it was to create drama that I did it."

When Madonna arrived in Italy she made a speech to the Vatican about the importance of freedom of artistic expression. "The Italians typically over-reacted ... they put all this propaganda in the Italian newspapers to try and put kids off coming. It really hurt me because I'm Italian ... It was like a slap in the face. I felt incredibly unwelcome there. And misunderstood. Apart from anything else it was completely sexist."

While the Catholic church considers masturbation to be a mortal sin, Madonna feels it's a simple form of self-love, and an exploration of your own sexuality. "I think a lot of people would rather not admit that it's a big part of everybody's life. I obviously am not afraid to admit that... if it's out in the open in my show, then perhaps the kids who

Above: **The pony tail made its debut during the 'Blond Ambition' tour, along with the ever present crucifix and artifacts of Catholicism used during the 'confessional' sequences.**

Facing page: **Madonna strips for photographers at the Cannes Film Festival, 1990. Her dramatic entrance upstaged leading stars and led to suggestions that she hi-jacked the entire event for self-publicity.**

"When Madonna at Cannes parted the crowds and, amid flashbulbs, stripped down to her underwear, no one was much surprised. She's like that. But if nice girls on the Paris catwalks dress up their petticoats with patent gloves and boots that seem to have party not boudoir in mind, it's time to go public about lingerie. The way bedroom secrets have moved on to the street must be the fashion phenomenon of our times."
Vogue, October 1991.

watch will lose any fear of it they have."

Puritanical Toronto police threatened to close Madonna's show and arrest her if she so much as touched her crotch, obviously unaware that such an ultimatum was like a red rag to a bull in Madonna's case. She stubbornly refused to tone down her show, even if it meant spending a night in some uncomfortable Canadian jail house. "I went on and of course was more obscene than I could ever imagine... after all it's a theatrical performance. It's not like I'm going out in the street running around without my clothes on." In the end, Madonna believes the police must have seen the irony in her show, because no arrest was made.

She was equally adamant with her father when he asked her to keep things clean on the night that he was going to be in the audience. In a touching scene from her documentary film, Madonna talks to him on the phone and warns: "It's pretty racy in some sections, I don't know if you could take it two nights in a row." But won't she tone it down – just a bit – for him? "No," Madonna asserts. "Because that would be compromising my artistic integrity."

Nobody under the age of 18 was legally allowed to see the film *In Bed With Madonna* because of its sexual content but they could read all about it in the papers: Madonna flashing her breasts at the camera; Madonna simulating oral sex with a bottle; Madonna romping around in bed with one of her naked dancers and commenting on the size of his dick; Madonna embarrassing an old girlfriend by talking about their childhood sex play (the friend denies it when interviewed separately). While the imagination runs riot when reading about these incidents, in reality it was all just good rude fun, Madonna-style.

"The film embarrasses me a little at times," admits Madonna. "But if it was going to be any good, it would have to, don't you think?" She hoped her father would appreciate her efforts when he finally got around to seeing it. "This is a movie that takes a while to digest... I think at first he will be shocked by it, but I think he will understand and ultimately approve of it."

Madonna is aware that her sexual image looms in front of her wherever she goes, that people have lewd expectations of her and that many a man would find her a frightening proposition. "Everyone probably thinks that I'm a raving nymphomaniac, that I have an insatiable sexual appetite, when the truth is I'd rather read a book." But it's an image she enjoys keeping up with her consistently saucy quips.

Madonna once said her ultimate goal was to rule the world. When asked if she would like to consider running for President on the BBC Omnibus documentary, she giggled. "No, because I've had too much sex. You're not allowed to have sex and run for office so I don't think it's a possibility."

FAME & POWER

Speculation abounds as to how much Madonna and her mighty empire are worth, but she is certainly one of the richest women in the world, and her fortune now runs into hundreds of millions. She has properties in New York, Los Angeles and Miami; a substantial collection of serious art; and in 1992 she struck a $60 million deal with Warners for her own multi-media entertainment company, Maverick. This prospering artistic 'think-tank' intends to branch into films, television, videos and books, and boasts one of the few artist-run record labels to have reached the big-league status.

"Do you know how much money you have in the bank?" a deejay once asked on a radio interview. To which Madonna replied, "No, and furthermore, when people talk about how much money I make, they talk about my gross, not like after I pay off all my bills - my managers, my agents and my taxes. Let's just say I'm comfortable."

Madonna's motivation to be rich and famous came from a wealth of handicaps: from living in the smelly industrial town of Bay City ("I had a great desire and need to get out of that small town kind of feeling and go somewhere and be somebody"); from being raised in a large family of eight brothers and sisters ("There's that competitiveness that you have when there's a whole bunch of you"); from her father's disciplinarian ways, which allowed for no idle time; and from her mother's untimely death.

Madonna has said that from childhood she always behaved as if she were a star. "I don't think it was a trait many people appreciated... I think I was incredibly precocious and a pain in the arse." She has also said that if her mother was alive today, she probably wouldn't be in the entertainment business at all. "Her death changed me, it turned me into the warrior that I am because it hurt me so deeply." Madonna decided to become an over-achiever in order to get approval from the world. "All of a sudden I was going to become the best student, the best singer, the best dancer, the most famous person... everybody was going to love me."

Madonna also feels she lacks the feminine touch in terms of good manners, gentleness and patience, because her mother wasn't around to teach her these qualities. Instead she developed a tough skin and an aggressive demeanour. Desperate for global affection, Madonna took her first step by leaving home against her father's will. "Since I was 17 and moved to New York, I haven't needed my father's help."

Strangely enough, nobody in her school was that surprised when Madonna made it big, even though the odds were stacked against a young girl from a remote suburban community becoming so phenomenally famous. Such was her charisma that when her dream came true everyone simply accepted it.

The art of control came easily to Madonna as she began to take the reins and manoeuvre her way to the top via her own smarts. "While it might have seemed like I was behaving in a stereotypical way, at the same time I was also mastermind-

"Power is the great aphrodisiac…and I'm a very powerful person."

Facing page: **Madonna apes Marilyn Monroe's famous 'Diamonds Are A Girl's Best Friend' sequence from the film 'Gentlemen Prefer Blondes'.**

ing it. I was in control of everything I was doing." But power was something she had yet to discover. After years of being in charge, Madonna was taken by surprise when *Playboy* and *Penthouse* released the famous nude photographs of her in 1985, and she had to face the whole world at the Live Aid concert while the scandal was still fresh. "People were screaming, 'Take it off, take it off'... and I really wasn't sure of myself. So I decided to be a warrior and it worked, and that was the first time that I really understood my power."

Despite all the comparisons with Marilyn Monroe, Madonna's tight grip on her own destiny ensures that the resemblance is only skin deep. As Madonna has always said, "Monroe was a victim and I'm not."

Greil Marcus made this comment on the BBC Omnibus programme: "After about five years of her career Madonna was probably the most famous woman in the world. She didn't have a nervous breakdown... she didn't become a junkie. She did get married but who went crazy? Her husband! She didn't go crazy. She seems to have been born for fame, for pressure that usually breaks people."

Madonna is a self-confessed control freak and believes that this obsession is the key to her sanity. "I have to schedule everything. Friends say to me, 'Can't you just wake up in the morning and not plan your day? Can't you just be spontaneous?' And I just can't." Order and organisation calm the maelstrom of Madonna's crazy life. Routine and ritual weave a safety net to catch her if she falls. There is the comfort of a time for everything and everything is in its proper place.

The extent of this obsession was revealed in an interview with *Vanity Fair*, when a journalist asked Madonna to think of a most recent happiest moment. Madonna replied, "Right after the maid has left for the day. That's my favourite time in the world. Everything's perfect – no-one's allowed on the bed and I just stand around and look. And I think I'm in a church, that I'm surrounded by holiness."

Madonna doesn't count sheep when she can't sleep, she makes lists of all the things she needs to do the next day, and people she needs to call. "I sleep a certain number of hours every night. Then I like to get up and get on with it. I set aside the three hours I have to make phone calls. Then I set aside the hours I have to exercise. The I set aside the hours for creativity... I can summon my creativity."

And should some mortal emotion dare to pierce the stubborn metal of this warrior's armour such as an involuntary mood of anguish or despair, Madonna will call upon her head to rule her heart. There is no time to wallow in self-pity. "I allow myself a 24 hour mourning period. Then I snap out of it so I can get on with everyday life. Maybe deep down inside I'm not over it. But for all intents and purposes, it appears that I am."

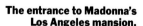

The entrance to Madonna's Los Angeles mansion.

With so much order, restraint and self-discipline in her life, it is clear that Madonna has to have some equally extreme form of release. Anonymous ex-friends have said that she is mad, bad and embarrassing to know when she is out on the town with her support group of girlfriends. Madonna and her sisterhood have been rudely nicknamed the 'Snatch Batch' with Madonna as the leader of the Batch. She is said to let off steam by staging belching contests in restaurants or getting everyone to order the same meal and then eating it with their fingers.

Madonna pleads guilty to some of the charges made against her. "I'm a brat for sure but I don't travel in a pack... certainly I can be a bitch. I'm a perfectionist, and I'm under lots of pressure. Sometimes you have to be a bitch to get things done... I can be something of a tyrant. In a working situation. Well, in a living situation too."

She has a reputation for being a tough and impatient interviewee. When Madonna fields questions that are either uncomfortable or just plain ludicrous – Whose baby would you like to have? Could you ever go back to being what you were before you became a star? – she reacts like the mythical Medusa: fixing her interviewer with a look that could turn them to stone, or rolling her eyes to the heavens in a gesture of open despair.

She has the ability to strike fear into the hearts of veteran chat show hosts. Not surprisingly, the avuncular Terry Wogan went all bashful on Madonna when they met in Cannes. "Are people afraid of you?" he asked from the safety of his chair, which had been positioned an imperial distance away from the sofa in which Madonna languished; no cosy knee-to-knee communion with this guest. "I'm very confrontational," she replied. "I think it's hard for people to hide from me when they meet me."

But this tyrannical reputation has created a monster with which Madonna no longer wants to be identified. She silenced her manager's protests against the candid nature of *In Bed With Madonna* by pointing out that... "Everyone already thinks I'm a bitch. They already think I'm Attila the Hun. They already compare me to Adolf Hitler and Saddam Hussein." Madonna hoped the film would help to shatter this exaggerated myth. "I think a great deal of the movie shows a gentler side of me. I think what you see is not a control freak but someone who has to hold the whole ship together. I really have to be a rock."

Madonna has no qualms about her love of power. In these backward days of so-called equality when it is still considered unseemly for a woman to be the boss – when a powerful man is hailed as 'ambitious' but a powerful woman merely inspires a torrent of back-stabbing abuse – Madonna asks us to be honest with ourselves and admit that power is "the quest of every human being."

Power is a pure and simple affair for Madonna. It is a strength we should all cultivate in order to

With new-found wealth, Madonna has adopted the sophisticated habits that a carefree lifestyle permits. She is a collector of modern art; she is a lover of classical music and good literature; and she's fond of fine furniture. Her lifestyle means she'll live long enough to enjoy her success.

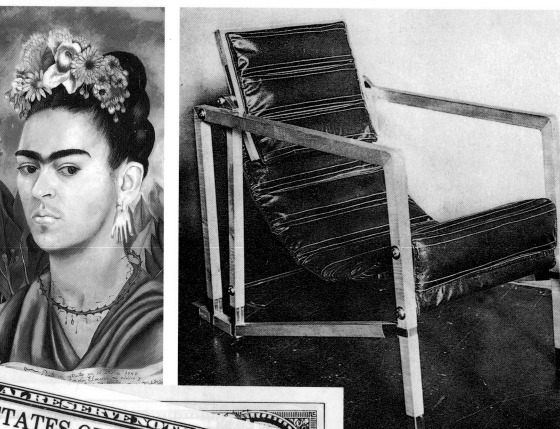

Left: **Is she the richest woman in rock. During 'Material Girl' on the 'Virgin' tour Madonna distributed her own currency to the audience to prove she wasn't materialistic after all.**

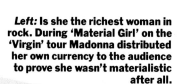

Top left: **New York's Guggenheim Museum. Art collector Peggy Guggenheim is one of Madonna's role models.**
Top right: **Picasso is among the artists collected by Madonna, along with Salvador Dali and other surrealists.**
Above left: **A self-portrait by Mexican painter Frida Kahlo, Madonna's favourite artist.**
Above: **Eileen Gray's Transat chair. Madonna has a valuable collection of Art Deco furniture.**

INFLUENCES &

Health and efficiency: Madonna has adopted a tough physical fitness regime in which biking plays a big part and cycling shorts are an essential fashion item.

Home listening: Madonna's personal record collection includes Bach, Mozart and Handel's 'Water Music'. She prefers to listen to classical music rather than Hi-NRG on the rare occasions when she gets a chance to relax.

Essential reading: James Joyce, Ernest Hemingway and Jack Kerouac are Madonna's favourite authors.

Stoned or stoneground: Madonna has chosen a healthy, wholemeal life-style in contrast to the auto-destruct image of her megastar predecessors; greens instead of grass, carrots instead of cocaine, lentils instead of liqueur.

ES/PART4

feel good about ourselves. Madonna's interpretation of power is a far cry from the inflated ego trip of the male definition. It doesn't throw its weight around or tread on other people in order to make them look small. It is merely a matter of self-respect. "Anyone can have power, it's how you feel about yourself, it's how you carry yourself, it's the effect that you have on people."

And Madonna is quick to point out that power is not the same thing as 'fame' at all. "Being a star is about being fabulous," she teases. "Being in the spotlight, having your picture taken all the time and having everyone worship and adore you; being rich, rich, rich and having it all."

Madonna the glamorous superstar may have become just another pin-up with 'big boobies' for heterosexual men; but Madonna the astute business woman is the first heroine to come complete with balls, as far as body conscious feminists are concerned. Her brains and uncommon beauty have merged to form a rare partnership indeed. Madonna is no passive, shallow starlet. "I ultimately end up making my own work. I don't sit around waiting for other people to give it to me."

President and matriarch of a business empire that recycles some of her earnings back into her work, Madonna is involved with every decision from dull paperwork to creativity. "I'm a detail freak. I know everything that's going on... although it's hard for me to sit with my business manager and stay interested for very long in money issues."

"She's a great business woman," says Seymour Stein, President of Sire Records. "She's very smart and she trusts her instincts, which are great. She also asks a million questions."

"I'm impulsive and I don't mull things over," confirms Madonna. "And when I make big mistakes... they're glaring. Then I have to eat humble pie."

Madonna is directly responsible for hundreds of jobs and, naturally, most of her key employees are women. The wanton company titles she has adopted for her various projects laugh in the face of sexism by revelling in derogatory terms. "Boy Toy is for my music. Siren is my film company and Slutco is for my videos... there is a wink behind everything I do."

It is hard to imagine what it must be like to work for this demanding woman who makes it clear that, "I do what I want. I'm the boss." It's easy to envisage a caricature image of Madonna the sadistic mistress, cracking her whip and handing out terrible punishments to minions whose efforts fall short of her exacting standards.

When Wogan asked, "What do you do to people who disagree with you?" Madonna rolled her eyes to the heavens and replied sarcastically, "What do I DO to them? I have them sentenced to jail and I have their heads cut off." Madonna's manager jokes that when they have a disagreement, "She has a doll and she squeezes it in all the right places, and I feel pain."

In reality, however, everyone from her assistant to her lawyer is part of a close knit family of carefully chosen friends to whom Madonna turns for constructive criticism. "I feel the most nervous around people who can't be honest with me and who can't look me in the eye." Part of Madonna's success is having faith in this family and listening to their advice. "To have total control means you can lose objectivity. What I like is to be surrounded by really talented, intelligent people I can trust and ask them for their input."

Freddie DeMann and Seymour Stein are the parental figures in this family. Like her real father, they will often throw up their arms in horror and disapprove of Madonna's more outlandish ideas upon first hearing. "There's always the preliminary shit that's thrown, and then there's my 'shit-fit' and then I do what I have to do... and then they like it."

What so many people admire about Madonna is the way that she works so hard for everything she has. "She is the most determined person I know and the most driven," boasts her brother Christopher. "I know a lot of people in the industry and she works a hundred times harder than all of them. Work is her ritual, it's like breathing for the rest of us. It's sort of unnatural in a way."

Warren Beatty, normally a man of few words, had eloquent praise for Madonna's unrivalled level of commitment. "The most surprising thing about her after I had worked with her was to see the level of diligence that she has. She works really hard... I don't know that there are many people who can do as many things as Madonna can do as well; who bring as much energy and willingness to work as Madonna does."

Catholicism and a disciplinarian father drummed the hard work ethic into Madonna's conscience: you can't have happiness unless you struggle and sweat for it. Many of her comments give this attitude away. "I believe that you can't have lasting happiness unless you have actually worked hard for your reward. The bigger you want to do things and the more a perfectionist you are, you have to work 24 hours a day... sometimes I think I don't enjoy my success enough or I don't have enough time to just kick back and have a good time... I'm exhausted and I wish I wasn't so tired. But you can't have things this good unless you work for it."

When asked on the BBC Omnibus programme why she pushed herself so hard, Madonna replied: "Because I have demons. Because I wanna live for ever, because when I die I don't want people to forget that I existed. Because I'm constantly looking for the truth in life... because I have so much energy that if I sat around for too long I'd probably explode."

Not only doesn't she give herself time to enjoy her success, Madonna also feels awkward about her embarrassment of riches. "I have a completely guilty conscience about the fact that I have money, so I'm always giving it away."

During the London leg of the 'Blond Ambition' tour Madonna jogs past Buckingham Palace, a piece of real estate beyond even her economic grasp.

T. WOGAN (for it is he): Tonight I celebrate my millionth programme by interviewing perhaps the biggest female star of all time, the most famous woman in the world. Ladies and gentlemen – Madonna.
(Camera tracks away to reveal huge golden throne surrounded by cherubim, seraphim, etc, in adoring poses.)
WOGAN (taking seat on small passing cloud): Madonna, you've been at the top now for nearly 2000 years. Most people would agree that you are the ultimate superstar. You've got everything you have ever wanted – fame, millions of devoted fans, you're a role model for young girls all over the world. And yet there are those who wonder whether you are trapped by this phenomenal success that you've had. I mean, would you have thought, when you were ordinary and unknown like any other kid on the block that one day you'd have all this power, and success, and fame? So, you're liberated, and you didn't feel you had to get married when you had that much-publicised relationship with Warren Beatty (surely 'Joseph'? Ed) but what I really want to know is (contd p. 94)
Private Eye magazine, August 1991.

She has always denied being a material girl. In 1984, when success was still a novelty experience, Madonna said: "Money's not important. I never think I want to make millions and millions of dollars." She even seemed to begrudge her impending wealth. "The more money you have the more problems you have... life was simpler when I had no money, when I just barely survived."

In 1985, when success was assured, Madonna's only possessions were a bicycle stored in New York, a Persian carpet stored in Los Angeles, and two old trunks of clothing which she kept on her tour bus. But now she had to concede that, "Money's a gas! I lived in New York for years and it was such a struggle, and it's so much more of a pleasure to be there now... at the same time, if I lost it all, it wouldn't be the end of the world because I could still work and I'd still have me. I'm not a materialistic person."

Nowadays Madonna will tell you that..."Having money is just the best thing in the world" but only because..."It gives you freedom and power and the ability to help other people." She also has an irrational fear that..."someone will come and take it all away from me. That makes me work really hard all the time."

"She's one of the least materialistic people I know," says Madonna's brother Christopher. "She's the paradox of it I suppose."

So what does a reluctant millionairess spend her money on? "I buy art and invest money in good scripts, and give it to people who need it." Madonna enjoyed bestowing gifts upon the unworldly dancers she had chosen to appear with her on the Blond Ambition tour. "I could show them things and be a mother to them. Take care of them. Assuage my guilt for having so much money by taking them shopping at Chanel and buying them everything their hearts desired... it makes me feel better for a while."

She financed her own video extravaganza for the 'Express Yourself' single to the tune of almost a million dollars. At the time she simply said, "I've basically gone wildly out of control. My manager gets insane about what I spend. But it placates me to put my energy into that work. I could be buying a Ferrari, but I'd rather spend it this way."

"She doesn't like to throw money away on frivolous things," confirms her fitness instructor and constant companion Rob Parr. "She has one car, no grand jewellery - just simple pieces. A nice house in Los Angeles and an apartment in New York, but they're not grand."

Madonna's only real material indulgence is for art; she is now counted among America's top collectors and said to be a most discriminating buyer of modern art, vintage photographs, art deco and art nouveau, hunting out new things wherever she goes. "There was this point in my life when I wanted to be Peggy Guggenheim - be this patron of artists - to have a gallery and a great art collection. When I'm really, really old, that's what I want to do. Peggy Guggenheim had a wild life. I like that."

Mexican art is something Madonna champions, especially the female painter Frida Kahlo, a legendary artist and revolutionary whose life she plans to make into a film one day. One of Kahlo's paintings is a bizarre self-portrait of herself being born; emerging from between her mother's legs - not as a baby - but as a fully grown adult. Bloody, bizarre and shocking, Madonna says mysteriously: "If somebody doesn't like this painting then I know they can't be my friend."

Madonna's homes are frequently described as being modest and unostentatious. Her LA home is humble by Hollywood standards; a comfortable but inconspicuous place in Los Feliz, a trendy neighbourhood that nestles between Hollywood and downtown LA. (She had to move out of her former home in the Hollywood Hills because she was being bothered there by a disturbing persistent stalker).

Madonna prefers to live in Miami, where she has a small and anonymous house in Coconut Grove, and a boat called Baby Pumpkin, from where she can feed the local dolphins. Her Miami living room was designed by her younger brother Christopher and is decorated in a French Deco style. When a journalist from *The Face* visited this house, she described it thus: "The house is beautiful... in a simple way. The arched doorways are picked out in fossilised local coral, the main ceiling is panelled wood. The furniture is tasteful, minimal and comfortable: big cream sofas sprinkled with fat cushions, church candles everywhere, dark wood in the 12-seater dining room. Downstairs is mainly open-plan, with a large, cool living room leading to a formal dining room at one end, an office/TV room at the other, and doors opening out into the garden... The impression is neat, ordered, free of clutter, but lived in too - this is no showcase home."

In New York, Madonna's seven-room Manhattan apartment reflects the simplicity and lavishness of her Miami home full of French deco furnishings, chosen by her brother Christopher, and cubist art. Not many people can boast that they have a genuine Picasso and an equally genuine Dali hanging in their home; Madonna can. And as you would expect, she also has the most organised wardrobe in town, with tidy rows of shoes and neatly hung clothes. Madonna says of her apartment: "It has the feel of a refuge, a controlled, beautiful environment where dirt is a memory and each detail is perfect."

The sanctity of Madonna's surroundings is echoed in the music she plays. "I love Mozart and Chopin. My favourite music is baroque, Vivaldi and Bach and Handel's 'Water Music'." In her previous spare time she reads and entertains. Madonna's idea of a holiday is... "a weekend when I don't have to do any work. I go to the movies, drink Martinis and have dinner parties... I love to gobble up books and poetry and biographies. I

"The best thing about the nineties is its secure femininity. Women can express their womanliness and are no longer afraid to accentuate the bellybutton, the waist and the hips. Strong women are not afraid to be proud of their breasts." **Stefano Gabbana of Dolce and Gabbana, Italy's controversial design duo who have championed the bustier.**

"Superman displays superiority over his fellow men by wearing his underpants on the outside of his clothes. Today's superwoman shows hers by wearing no outer garments at all. That at least is the message of this week's fashion collections in Milan... the catwalk swarmed with suspenders and stocking-tops, wasp-waisted corsets and tassled bras, see-through chiffon, stiletto heels and elbow-length gloves, a mocking touch of prudery amid the rudery." **Daily Mail, October 1991.**

THE MEN &

Above, from top: **Madonna at a New York party with photographer friend Steve Meisel; with DJ/dance producer John Benitez, better known as Jellybean, with whom Madonna enjoyed a romantic relationship in 1983; and with her favourite brother Christopher, a regular backstage VIP on Madonna's tours.**

Right: **The Breakfast Club rehearsing in New York in 1979. Playing drums is Madonna's former New York boyfriend Dan Gilroy who taught her the rudiments of music 'She was a maniac for rehearsing,' says Gilroy. 'She was a real workaholic.'**

Above: **Madonna and Warren Beatty arrive at a party at Herb Ritts' studio in August, 1989. The following April, seemingly happier to be behind the wheel, she drives Michael Jackson to a West Hollywood restaurant.**

THE BOYS...

Madonna has made no secret of her liking for men. First it was the cute Puerto Rican boys in New York, then the musicians who taught her dance grooves and then the best that Hollywood could throw at her. Who will finally capture Madonna's heart...?

Above: Madonna's father, Sylvio Ciccone.
Right: Riding the Pacific Coast Highway with trainer in 1987.
Below: With ex-husband Sean Penn in 1987. Theirs was one of the shorter Hollywood marriages.

Sire Records boss Seymore Stein who signed Madonna while in a bed at Lennox Hill Hospital, New York. 'I shaved. I combed my hair. I even got a new dressing gown'.

Left: On Broadway with girlfriend Sandra Bernhard during Madonna's run in the play 'Speed The Plow' in 1988.

Far left: With dancer and occasional beau Tony Ward in the erotic 'Justify My Love' video in which Madonna submits to all manner of advances.

love the classics: James Joyce, Henry James, Hemingway, D. H. Lawrence, Jack Kerouac... man I love to read."

Madonna rarely allows herself the luxury of a proper holiday. She would rather squeeze every second out of life and invest it with productivity than languish on some exotic beach. "I've taken three vacations in the last ten years, all of them lasted about a week... my boyfriend or husband at the time would want to go and I'd agree. Actually, I've finally given in."

Madonna has been blessed with an abundance of energy and gets by on very little sleep. It is of paramount importance to be of sound mind and body to keep up the pace. Drugs hold no attraction and... "drinking Martinis is about as out of control as I will ever get." Her idea of true relaxation is to run six or more miles a day. "It's a time when

I meditate, so spiritually it's great for me. It's when I tune everything out, all the problems, all the stress, all the demands, all the expectations. I just run. It sounds corny but it's zen-like, it's the time I escape so it does me a lot of good."

And yet, beyond this fragile veneer of order and tranquillity, Madonna will tell you that... "my life remains completely insane. Don't let this calm, peaceful façade fool you." Her family is her only lifeline to reality. One of the reasons why Madonna likes to go home to visit her father is that he insists on treating her like her brothers and sisters – as an ordinary person. Sometimes it frustrates her that he doesn't seem to realise what a star she has become, but at least it's the one place in the whole world where she can regress to being a nobody again.

Madonna still has a handful of friends from the

Unquestionably the spiritual heir to Monroe, Madonna stresses one important difference between her and Marilyn: Madonna is in charge of her own destiny.

days when she first moved to New York... "and of course they're my best friends... they remained true and deep friends all these years no matter what's happened to me." She doesn't feel any natural affinity towards other celebrities just because she is one herself. In a poignant scene from *In Bed With Madonna*, when Sandra Bernhard asks her who she'd really like to meet next, Madonna replies sadly, "I think I met everybody." When she's playing the game of Truth Or Dare with her dancers and one of them asks who the biggest love of her life is, she confesses that it's still her ex-husband, Sean Penn.

Madonna hides her loneliness with her commando attitude and by becoming deeply embroiled with other people's problems so that she can forget her own. When she watched back the footage from her Blond Ambition tour, she was surprised to see how maternal her behaviour was towards her brothers and her dancers, that she was... "the matriarch of all these little families." Film maker Alex Keshishian described her as... "a post modern mother to a bunch of wayward kids." But every now and then Madonna says she breaks and needs someone to take care of her. The need to dominate and be in charge is pushed aside for the need to be loved.

"It's something of a cliché, but you can have all the success in the world and if you don't have someone to love, it's certainly not as rewarding. The fulfilment you get from another human being will always dwarf people recognising you on the street."

The poor-little-rich-girl-lonely-at-the-top syndrome is something every journalist loves to quiz Madonna about when they interview her. She will honour their prying questions with the same honesty that is expected in a game of Truth Or Dare, sometimes blinking back tears that she just can't seem to hide.

"I long for children. I wish that I was married and in a situation where having a child was possible. But first I have to find a man and that's more difficult than you might suppose... how do I find a man who likes me for myself? If you are in my position, you trust but you are often let down." Madonna has no intention of raising a child alone. "I want a father there. I want someone to depend on." A close friend recommended a good female psychiatrist to Madonna. The sessions were of some comfort. I don't know if going to a shrink helps your loneliness but it sure helps you understand it."

Madonna always insists that she is hopeful, and that "time hasn't run out for me yet." But as 1990 gave way to 1991 and Madonna held a New Year's Eve party in her Hollywood home, a disturbing event took place that filled her with despair. A guest claiming to be a palm reader shocked Madonna with her gloomy predictions. "She said I'm never going to have any children. She said that I had my heart broken really badly once... and it was going to happen again. I asked her about my career and she said, 'Whatever you're working on now, you're not well suited for'... I was devastated. That woman said things that made me believe her." Madonna got drunk on just two Martinis and passed out on her marble bathroom floor. "First time in my life I got sick. I lost control. And I missed my party."

Madonna had enjoyed the constancy of married life. Even the domesticity. "When I was married, I did the wash a lot. I liked folding Sean's underwear. I liked mating socks... there's something to be said for a domestic life and knowing somebody's there for you."

Friends have said that Madonna's marriage to Sean was like the tempestuous love hate relationship that Elizabeth Taylor and Richard Burton shared, and that it was Madonna's drive and dedication towards her career that led to her and Sean's divorce. "I went through a period when I felt like a total failure, as any good Catholic girl would," remembers Madonna. "Time heals everything... it doesn't hurt so much anymore. It goes into another compartment."

It seemed like a match made in heaven when Madonna met Warren Beatty. Back in the sixties, he had been the male Madonna of his time; a Hollywood sex symbol with a seemingly insatiable libido. This legendary beau was well acquainted with the trials and tribulations of fame. He was Madonna's equal in terms of fame and financial clout.

"Warren understands the bullshit. He's been an icon for years. He's had a lot more practice at it than I have. Obviously somebody who hasn't experienced it would be more threatened by my fame than he is." But the romance fizzled out after the film's release. Friends have said that Madonna was too independent and stubborn for Beatty; witness the tense few scenes in which they appear together in her documentary film, scenes he wanted taken out but which Madonna insisted on keeping in. It has also been said that Beatty hurt Madonna by flirting with other women. It was unkindly suggested that Beatty merely used Madonna in order to promote a film in which he had a financial interest.

Looking back, Madonna wonders how things might have been if she had been less dominating and demanding. "If I had changed and given in to certain concessions that people had asked of me, maybe the relationships would have been successful on the one hand, but then I would have had to give up other things in my career. And then I would have been miserable."

Madonna the warrior continues to roam around her uncompromising world like a miniature tank, and yet she has endearingly confessed to deep feelings of insecurity. Friends have commented that the true Madonna is at odds with her public image, confused by her success and ill at ease with her superstar status as if she cannot keep up with the reality of everything that has happened to her.

Her manager once boasted that "Madonna is the biggest star in the universe, and she likes the view." But the sad and strange truth is that Madonna never allows herself to catch her breath long enough to rest up and enjoy the view. Every time she reaches a new peak, she pushes herself on towards the next one.

For while Madonna has succeeded in winning the attention of the world, she has yet to win her own self approval. She has revealed that her real drive in life comes from a fear of being mediocre. "I have an iron will, and all of my will has always been to conquer some horrible feeling of inadequacy. I'm always struggling with that fear. I push past one spell of it and discover myself as a special human being, and then I get to another stage and think I'm mediocre and uninteresting."

Madonna is learning to be less hard on herself. "I want to be happy. I have moments of happiness... I'm working towards knowing myself and I'm assuming that will bring me happiness... You see, I don't think you can truly be loved until you know and love yourself. Then you can be truly loved and that's what I want."

Although she sometimes found it difficult to watch herself and her behaviour in the film *In Bed With Madonna*, she has said that the experience was worth five years of psychoanalysis. Despite some painful moments, she really got to know herself. "I've learned to love myself more through this movie and to see that in the midst of all my ambition and desire to succeed and my search for approval, I do give things to people. I do bring some sort of happiness into their lives... I can see all my extreme behaviour, but I can also see my goodness."

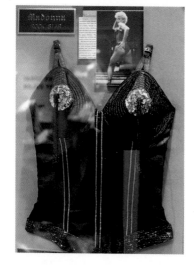

INTO THE NINETIES

Dita Parlo was a German silent movie actress of the 1930s, and Madonna, being an avid film buff, used this name whenever she checked into hotels around the world. She later assumed the actress's identity for what was to become her most notorious venture of all – a dirty coffee table book called *Sex*.

In 1992 and 1993 Madonna took centre stage for a tacky trilogy of projects that were guaranteed to shock and outrage, but mostly disappoint: the book called *Sex*, the video for her new single 'Erotica', and a film called *Body Of Evidence*. All three had one thing in common – an obsession with sado-masochism.

Up until now, Madonna's use of sexual imagery had always been subversively saucy and tongue-in-cheek: the "BOY TOY" belt; the white wedding dress for 'Like A Virgin'; the little black T-shirt that boasted "Italians Do It Better"; and the comical torpedo bras worn by the male dancers in her Blond Ambition tour.

But *Sex* was a dark project with little obvious humour – and there was something sinister about the creation of Dita Parlo.

Dita was a dominatrix who brandished a whip and peered menacingly from behind a black leather mask. She wore a long black razor-sharp false nail over her one of her fingers, and a gold cap tooth (inscribed with the letter "D") over one of her front teeth. When she spoke (at the beginning of the 'Erotica' single), Dita had the scratchy gravel voice of a woman who smoked too much. She rasped about pain and pleasure: "Only the one who hurts you can comfort you/Only the one who inflicts the pain can take it away." She wasn't someone you'd want to meet in a dark alley.

Sex was Madonna's first literary outing; a spiral-bound book of erotic musings and pictures that fell to bits after you'd leafed through it a few times – such was the poor design of the jacket. The musings were written by Madonna with the help of *Interview* journalist Glenn O'Brien, and the pictures were all shot by fashion photographer Steven Meisel.

Madonna's naked body features in a collection of soft-core pictures that are occasionally a little hard to swallow. The idea seemed to be a continuation of the "Flesh and Fantasy" portfolio that Meisel and Madonna had worked on together for *Rolling Stone* in June 1991.

In that issue, Madonna posed semi-naked for a series of pictures that were inspired by the work of a photographer called Brassai, who documented life in the sexual underworld of Paris during the Twenties and Thirties – focusing on brothels, cabarets, and gay and lesbian night clubs.

Madonna was anxious to make it clear that the scenes in *Sex* were not her own private fantasies; she was merely playing a role, much as any actress would in a movie. And this was a bit of a cop out. "I take on the persona of a character named Dita Parlo, she's the good-time girl, she's the narrator of the book... it's not me saying 'this is my life'. These are erotic short stories and erotic imaginings."

Madonna was also anxious to point out that voyeurs shouldn't try these fantasies at home – because they take place in an imaginary "perfect world". This was a world without AIDS and the need for safe sex. A world where people were responsible enough to indulge their darkest fantasies – without really hurting one another.

The book begins with a journey through the shady bondage clubs of New York – and ends with Madonna surfacing in Miami for some sex on the beach. Throughout the book, Madonna poses suggestively with girls... with guys... with gays... with a dog... with a man who is old enough to be her father... with actress Isabella Rossellini, model Naomi Campbell, and a p op star called Vanilla Ice.

"The arena that I choose to express myself is sexuality, and sexuality has always been a taboo subject. But I'm trying to change that."

"I will admit to being mildly disquieted by Sex... *nothing in the book is technically hard-core, but the milieu is in itself pornographic, and darkly pornographic."* **Martin Amis.**

Previous page: On stage, The Girlie Show at London's Wembley Stadium.

Facing page: December, 1996: the premiere of *Evita* in Los Angeles. Madonna at last attained her goal of becoming a fully-fledged dramatic actress.

Madonna typically sits with her legs wide apart and her breasts popping out of a variety of bondage tops; she masturbates and bites people's bums; she whips people and drips hot candle wax over their bare skin.

And she is the willing victim of two skin-headed lesbians who tie her to a chair and kiss her, while one of them holds a knife to her throat. "There is something comforting about being tied up," Dita writes on bondage. "Like when you were a baby and your mother strapped you in the car seat. She wanted you to be safe. It was an act of love."

Madonna strips off on the streets of Miami so that Meisel can capture the candid reactions on people's faces as she whips her knickers off in gas stations and pizza parlours. "People were constantly turning alarms on and calling the police, so we'd have to leave and go to the next place."

Madonna's favourite photograph is the one where she stands on a busy road in broad daylight, attempting to thumb down a lift. Her only fashion accessories are high heels, a smart little handbag, and a cigarette hanging out of her mouth. "I felt really free. It's the most unpermissible thing. You're not supposed to be out in public without your clothes on... I couldn't stop giggling; the looks on these people's faces when they would drive by. I just had the best time."

Throughout the book, Madonna writes a collection of cheap porno-style fantasies and various odes to her pussy, which naturally has nine lives. "I love my pussy, it is the complete summation of my life... My pussy is the temple of learning."

There is clearly an intention of humour in the book; some of the orgiastic romps are obviously ridiculous (Madonna ejaculating sun tan lotion from a bottle between her legs all over Naomi's prostrate body). But the preponderance of sneering expressions; pierced and tattooed bodies; grubby rooms and spiteful props (knives, studs, chains, whips and stiletto heels); the stark photography; and the brutal metal covers that form the jacket; all combine to create a disquieting photo essay. In the shadowy vault of Madonna's sexual imagination, there are some dark corners that you'd rather not visit – that you'd rather not have to retain in your memory log.

Madonna's launch party for *Sex* took place in New York on October 16 and was a flagrant and flagellant attempt to bring the decadence of the book to life. An orgy of thrusting S&M mayhem greeted guests as naked dancers simulated sex, and dominatrixes whipped everyone into a frenzy. It was even reported that live sex acts were taking place behind illicit peepholes. Life-size pictures from the book were either hung on walls or flashed on screens, while Madonna flounced around wearing a bizarre Heidi costume – breasts heaving over the top of an ultra low-cut milkmaid's dress – and clutching a fluffy toy lamb. If anything, Heidi was an even spookier creation than Dita. The *Sex* hype simultaneously reached its climax – and its anticlimax – when it was published at midnight on October 21. Nobody was sure what to make of it, or even how they were supposed to react to it.

As a unique and thought-provoking study of female pornography (clitoral versus phallic desire), *Sex* was a triumph. What are little girls' fantasies made of? Slugs and snails and puppy dogs' tails – forget the sugar and spice. Some straight men must have felt just a little uncomfortable with the predominance of homo-erotic imagery – with the realisation that some women get turned on by the idea of two men together – just as men have always had their lesbian dreams. And they may even have been a little irked to realise that women share these lesbian dreams.

Author Martin Amis, who flew to America to review the book, gave Madonna credit for the way that she had manipulated this medium: "*Sex* streaks like a bullet through the dark sky of female sexual fantasy. Erotica and pornography are male preserves, made by men for men; there is nothing out there for women, except the joke beefcake of *Playgirl*... Madonna may be onto something with *Sex*."

As a lesson in marketing hype, *Sex* was without equal. No one was allowed to see the book before it was published – unless they signed a legal agreement that swore them to secrecy.

And when the book finally hit the shops, delivered by security guards, it was sealed inside an aluminium bag that prevented punters from taking a free peak. (One journalist remarked that the packaging made it look like a boil-in-the-bag orgasm.) The reader was forced into the role of voyeur as he or she ripped the bag open and examined its contents. *Sex* was the biggest ever hardback launch – 750,000 copies went on sale in five countries, and every newspaper and magazine on the planet had something to say about it.

But as a career move *Sex* was an unmitigated disaster. Unwittingly competing with herself, Madonna pitched her porn book against her new *Erotica* album, and the latter got lost in the furore. The video for the 'Erotica' single featured Dita talking dirty: "Give it up/Do as I say/Give it up and let me have my way/I'll give you love/I'll hit you like a truck/I'll give you love/I'll teach you how to ****!" And there was some fairly shocking footage of the bondage scenes in *Sex*. Needless to say, the video was deemed to be far too steamy for daytime viewing.

When *Sex* was published, critics slammed the book as a desperate attempt to shock – an act of unbecoming narcissistic exhibitionism – and an irresponsible attempt to bring back the anything-goes sexual promiscuity of the Sixties. Psychotherapists, roped into writing analytical essays about "the meaning of the book", concluded that *Sex* was actually a public exorcism of Madonna's own sexual repression and tortured feelings of self-loathing.

But it didn't take a genius to figure out that a violent moral storm was brewing – one that could seriously damage Madonna's career.

"It is important to point out that, in the majority of the pictures, Madonna looks very beautiful indeed. Nothing, in all the great hoo-ha surrounding Sex, has been more laughable than the stampede of male commentators attesting to her "ugliness"... it's hard not to detect a certain fearfulness lurking behind these men's protestations. Aggressively expressed sexual indifference has always been the last refuge of an intimidated scoundrel." **The Independent, October 1992.**

Sharing a joke with the *enfant terrible* fashion designer Jean Paul Gaultier.

Facing page: **Jean Paul Gaultier and Madonna on the catwalk at his 1992 Los Angeles show.**

So why on earth did she do it? And, more to the point, why didn't anyone advise her against it? Was Madonna now so rich, so isolated, and so used to getting her own way, that no one could warn her about the consequences of such a controversial idea? Her old friend (now ex-friend), Sandra Bernhard scathingly suggested that "On some level, she's bored, and she has to do something to scare herself." And writer Paul Morley concluded: "It's the self-satisfied world of a super-celebrity who has become so famous because of her gutsy understanding of the confusing power of sex and its associated guilts that no one near her dare say, look darling, don't crawl around on all fours with that cucumber up your arse, that's got nothing to do with busting taboos and conventions, that's just daft."

But Madonna couldn't (wouldn't) see what all the fuss was about. She claimed that she was acting as a sexual crusader on a mission to make people confront and discuss their fears and phobias, and so encourage a live-and-let-live society. Far from promoting sexual abuse, she wanted to put an end to it. She argued that if we could all learn to accept each other, whatever our sexual preferences, then the world would be a kinder, more tolerant place. "The reason there is bigotry, and sexism, and racism, and homophobia, is fear. People are afraid of their own feelings... and I'm saying: It's OK to have this thought and this feeling."

Madonna hoped that *Sex* would act as a short, sharp burst of shock treatment in a sexually repressed world. "My thing is not for everybody to have more sex; my thing is to feel comfortable with who you are, whether you are gay or you are straight or whatever. To not feel repressed and to not feel afraid... you don't get what you want unless you say what you want."

But it was the abundance of aggressive images in *Sex* that made Madonna's "love thy neighbour" argument so hard to accept. One picture in particular had everyone up in arms. A rape scene – made all the more horrifying by the fact that Madonna (dressed as a Catholic schoolgirl) looked as if she was enjoying her ordeal as two boys held her down and ripped off her clothes in a gymnasium. It was easy to see why so many people thought that the book was condoning violence against women. And this from a feminist icon!

In defence of the rape scene, Madonna argued that the picture wasn't really a rape scene at all, because the girl was allowing it to happen. "I'm playing the coquette, the virgin, and they are the bad boys. They take me, but only because I give them the opportunity to." She also made the startling confession that she had once been raped herself, and knew only too well that rape was not an experience that should be glamorised. "It happened to me a long time ago so over the years I've come to terms with it. In a way it was a real eye-opening experience. I'd only been in New York for a year and I was very young, very trusting of people... that experience completely turned me round

in terms of becoming much more street smart and much more savvy. Although it was devastating at the time, I know that it made me a much stronger person in retrospect. It forced me to be a survivor."

When asked why she was so obsessed with S&M, Madonna claimed that all Catholics were masochists because they were brought up to believe that pain and suffering can absolve you of your sins. "When I was growing up, there were certain things people did for penance; I know people that slept on coat hangers or kneeled on uncooked rice on the floor and prayed for hours... There was some ecstasy involved in that. And the whole thing of crucifixion – the idea of being tied up. It's surrendering yourself to someone. I'm fascinated by it. There's a lot of pain-equals-pleasure in the Catholic Church."

As a book designed "to provoke debate about sexuality", *Sex* succeeded in whipping up press hysteria on a global scale, as journalists looked desperately for the deeper meanings that Madonna promised them were there, and tried to make sense of the mixed messages.

Was it fantasy or filth? Was it porn dressed as art? Art dressed as porn? Or was it just a pop star undressed? Any sympathetic reactions came mainly from female journalists. In response to a picture of Madonna standing naked on a radiator and peering out of the shutters in a hotel room, Sarah Kent from *Time Out* magazine said: "I see Madonna as a prisoner, occasionally breaking the bonds of fame by leaping naked into the light of day and photographing the brief moment of release, before beating a hasty retreat to the safety of a dark-windowed limo."

In the London *Evening Standard*, Nigella Lawson made the point that "Madonna has always been a girl's girl. From the pubescent wannabes to her pop-culture chroniclers, her constituency is decidedly female. And here is Madonna, then, declaring that the fit subject for female pornography is not some pec-pumping beefcake but the woman herself... the role of woman as the subject of her own sexual fantasy is a fitting model for post-feminist porn."

And Suzanne Moore from *The Guardian* commented, "What is shocking about these pictures... is the extent to which Madonna wants to turn herself into an object. Yet, like the powerful men who go to prostitutes to have ashtrays tipped over them, this is only ever a fantasy of powerlessness. You never really forget for one minute that Madonna, even bound and gagged, is still Madonna in control, is still getting what Madonna wants."

Madonna found herself skating on thin ice as she began to field questions about *Sex*. In the interviews that followed, she was genuinely not prepared for the kind of grilling she would get over the content of her book.

As journalists lined up to give her the third degree, she became increasingly irritated when probed about the issues of pornography and violence. As far as Madonna was concerned, her disclaimer that these fantasies took place in an "ideal world" should have been enough to deflect any criticism. And this was naïve. American *Vogue* magazine commented that "She seems wilfully oblivious to the fallout from all this nipple flashing... She doesn't seem to have any sense of how her images can overwhelm her words, how she leads people on visually."

Even Madonna's die-hard fans felt alienated by *Sex*. Her teenage following, who were too young to buy the book but saw it any way, found the whole thing alarmingly distasteful.

While they had loved her earlier incarnations as a bra-flashing brazen pop tart, few of them had the stomach for Madonna's "full Monty" striptease. And the feminists who had adopted Madonna as their icon, found her degrading images a betrayal of all the faith that they had invested in her.

An article in *Newsweek* accused Madonna of "pitching the book to its enemies at the expense of its friends". When journalist Andrew Neal challenged Madonna about her responsibility towards her young fans she snapped, "My responsibility is to myself as an artist, OK." And in an interview with *Vogue* she dismissed her teenage following with a cruel lash of her tongue by saying, "Let's face it, they're not that bright."

But Madonna's fans were a little more perceptive than she gave them credit for. A 15-year-old "ex-fan" called Emma Forrest, writing for the *Evening Standard*, announced that "The teenage girls for whom Madonna was invented have moved on, wondering why their idol has chosen to put so much distance between herself and them...We only stayed because she promised to shock. Now she's taken everything off...what's left to hold our attention?" Emma and friends denounced *Sex* as "the desperate initiative of a woman who has allowed her image and her industry to overtake her music." And this was a vital point. What had happened to Madonna's music? *Erotica* was a fine album, but it had been thoroughly usurped by *that* book, and sales were poor compared to past offerings.

It was beginning to look as if Madonna had one more mission in mind – to extinguish her humble "pop star" origins and exalt herself as an "artist". Now that she had become the subject of so many feminist writings, university lectures, and even a book of dreams (*I Dream of Madonna*), it looked as if she was beginning to take herself as seriously as the academics and intellectuals who worshipped at her shrine.

In this great cult of Madonna, there now seemed little room for good old-fashioned fun. For the moment, at least, her endearingly playful, self-mocking humour had been replaced with a puffed-up pride that kept everyone at arm's length.

Julie Burchill, writing for *The Sunday Times*, said, "There are two Madonnas, and the pity is, that the humourless American one is taking over from the raunchy Italian one... the Italian one was playful and intuitive; the American Madonna is crude and humourless... Madonna is no longer the cheeky little chancer whose one theory about sex seemed to be that if it felt good, you should do it; she has now, in a peculiarly boring American mode, bound up sex with issues of civil rights and artistic expression."

When asked why she described herself as an artist, rather than as an entertainer, Madonna replied, "Because I don't necessarily entertain. Sometimes I enrage, sometimes I provoke, sometimes I disgust people, sometimes I make people cry, sometimes I touch people, sometimes I make people laugh. An entertainer is a whole different thing; an entertainer doesn't necessarily deal with reality. It's someone to make you forget. It's like a drug, it's euphoric, and I think it has its place in the world. But that's not the only thing I do. I think I'm an educator – and I do think I'm an artist."

Part three of Madonna's S&M hat-trick was a substandard sexual thriller called *Body of Evidence*, a poor man's version of *Basic Instinct* directed by Uli Edel and released in 1993.

Madonna plays the role of a seductress called Rebecca Carlson, who enjoys rough sex, and stands accused of screwing her rich sugar daddy to death. Arrested as the murder weapon, Rebecca then sets out to seduce her defence lawyer, played by Willem Dafoe, in a series of explicit but laughable sex scenes – culminating with Madonna pouring hot candle wax over his genitalia.

The director said of Madonna, "She's a powerful lady. Sometimes you feel like a tamer with a she-lion in a cage. You have to force her to jump through this burning hoop, and there are just two possibilities. Either she'll jump through the ring of fire... or she'll kill you".

Madonna probably did try to kill Uli when the film came out. However sexy the plot may have looked on paper, it was a flop on screen. Writer Julie Burchill made this comment: "She shouldn't have made *Body of Evidence* – copying Sharon Stone, who made her own name copying Madonna, was not a smart move." And one film critic sneered, "It's not just that Madonna doesn't make an effective Sharon Stone; she does not make an effective Madonna."

Understandably, many thought that the film was connected in some way with Madonna's *Sex* book. "It's got nothing to do with my book" she balked, "And nothing to do with my album. I was an actress in it, I've got nothing to do with the content of it... it's not my personal statement the way the book is, or my album." All that was missing was the T-shirt.

Dita came back to haunt everyone in Madonna's new tour, *The Girlie Show*, which kicked off in London in September. Madonna's cruel jibes at her young fans had successfully managed to keep them away.

When she arrived at Heathrow airport, a meagre posse of three turned up to greet her, and the British Press gleefully concluded that Madonna was a "goner". However, her Wembley shows were a successful sell-out, and proved that her popularity

"For many people, the point at which Madonna went too far in her dance with notoriety was in publishing the photo-volume Sex. *Not only did the pre-hype and subsequent furore totally overshadow her most consistent and best LP to date,* Erotica... *but the strange mixture of emotions it provoked suggests that she badly misjudged the extent to which she could flout public opinion where sexual inhibitions and double-standards are concerned."* **The Times, October 1996.**

The Girlie Show takes to the stage.

Following pages: **Body talk... The Girlie Show.**

Above: Hippy muscial *Hair* was an obvious inspiration for some set pieces in The Girlie Show. *Right:* Madonna snapped by paparazzi during photo sessions for *Sex*.

"The point about Madonna, surely the reason that she has become an icon for so many girls and women, is that the kind of sexuality she has projected has been entirely selfish. It has not, as men always assume, been for them. Sure, they might have got off on it. Sure, she might get off on the idea of men masturbating over her photographs... but primarily what she has projected is female pleasure, female desire, female wanting."
The Guardian, October 1992.

had not diminished as much as the media liked to make out.

Gob-smacked audiences stared open-mouthed as they thought they saw Madonna make an explicit entrance by sliding suggestively down a pole wearing nothing but a G-string – but it was one of her dancers. The real Madonna rose from the stage dressed as the devilish Dita in a black sequinned outfit consisting of bra, waistcoat and hot pants, worn with fishnet tights and knee-high wet-look boots; her blond hair cut severely into the shortest of elfin crops.

However unpopular Madonna had become, one thing she proved with this tour was that she could still put on a show.

The usual mixture of high-camp theatrics and raunchy dance routines revolved loosely around a theme of Broadway shows and stars, including *Hair* (flares, afro wigs and orgiastic love-ins), *My Fair Lady* (smart high-society race-track outfits), and *Cabaret* (Minelli and Deitrich).

Elegant, energetic, sexy and witty, The Girlie Show was a triumph of entertainment and choreography. Best of all, it proved that Madonna's sense of humour was still, mercifully, intact. "If Madonna is on her way down," wrote the *Daily Express*, "It's a gentle descent. The world's best-marketed pop poseur will be around for a while yet."

1994 did not start well for Madonna. She disgraced herself by appearing on the David Letterman show and using the "F" word thirteen times. While Letterman damned Madonna for her outrageous behaviour, Madonna claimed that she had been stitched up like the proverbial kipper.

Chatting to her before the show, Letterman's writers had encouraged her to be a bad girl and poke fun at the chat show host by unleashing a barrage of insults; they said he'd be ready for it and would play along. "They gave me a list of insults, basically. So in my mind, he knew that that's what the game plan was, that we were going to f*** with each other on TV. I told some of the writers I was going to swear, and they went, 'OK, great. Do it, we'll "bleep" it and it'll be hysterical.'"

But as Madonna played the game, Letterman acted genuinely shocked and disgusted, saying, "Oh stop it! Will you stop? Ladies and gentlemen, turn down your volumes! She can't be stopped. There's something wrong with her." To which Madonna replied, "There's definitely something wrong with me – I'm sitting here!" The Press had a field day with this sorry betrayal, and accused Madonna of being sordid, depraved and unbalanced.

All this negative press and prudery was beginning to take its toll on Madonna; there was the constant insinuation that her career was well and truly over and, since her Letterman ordeal, that she had even lost her mind.

She had reached rock bottom – and her confidence had taken an almighty dent. In October, she released a new album called 'Bedtime Stories' and used it as a vehicle to get her wounded anger off her chest, and proclaim that she was not sorry for anything that she had done, and further more, that she was not done yet.

One of the songs, 'Human Nature', served as Madonna's defiant and definitive statement about the whole *Sex* scandal: "Did I say something wrong? Oops, I didn't know I couldn't talk about sex – (I musta been crazy)... I'm not sorry," runs the chorus. "You punished me for telling you my fantasies/I'm breaking all the rules I didn't make/I'm not your bitch, don't hang your shit on me." And on a track called 'Survival' she sang "I'll never be an angel/I'll never be a saint it's true/I'm too busy surviving/Whether it's heaven or hell/I'm gonna be living to tell/Here's my story/No risk no glory."

Madonna argued that she was a not-so innocent victim of a completely hypocritical society. Like Eve, she had proffered an apple, and everyone had tripped over themselves to take a bite. So why should she bear all the guilt? "I called my book *Sex* because it was a very provocative title and I knew people would buy it because of that. And I knew people would want to look at the pictures – and yet they denounced it at the same time, so I thought, that's a statement of our society in itself."

In an interview with *The Face*, Madonna declared that she was being punished for being a single female, for having power and money, and for having a sex life and admitting that she enjoyed it. "I feel I've been misunderstood. I tried to make a statement about feeling good about yourself and exploring your sexuality, but people took it to mean that everyone should go out on a f***fest and have sex with everyone, and that I was going to be the leader of that."

Determined as ever not to compromise her artistic integrity, Madonna appeared on the cover of *Esquire* magazine wearing a skimpy black rubber bikini with a diamond-studded dog collar round her neck. And she had had her body pierced – her nose and her oh-so-famous belly button were adorned with gold rings.

Author Norman Mailer conducted a rather ungentlemanly interview; he seemed obsessed with Madonna's genitals and kept asking her why she hadn't gone the whole hog and posed for some "beaver" shots in *Sex*. When Madonna argued that – if the book was so disappointing, then why did everyone buy it? – Mailer boldly replied, "Sales are irrelevant. There's no way it would not have sold. But the way you pay for it is in the crap you're running into now."

Years later, Madonna revealed the true purpose of *Sex*: "It was my own personal rebellion against my father, against the way I was raised, against the culture, against society, against everything. It was just a huge, massive act of rebellion." Of all the opinion pieces and analytical scribblings that had ever been written about *Sex* – it turned out that the psychotherapists had been right all along.

Madonna meets Mailer in the July 1994 issue of *Esquire*.

EVITA

The making of the film of Andrew Lloyd Webber and Tim Rice's *Evita* had been an on-off-on-off project for some 15 years, and, in her glory days, Madonna had been considered an obvious choice for the starring role of Eva Peron – the Argentine actress who rose from poverty to become a political icon.

But Madonna was no longer a likely candidate for the role. She had notched up so many disastrous films on her résumé (*Shanghai Surprise, Who's That Girl, Body of Evidence, Dangerous Game*), that she was on the verge of being relegated to that lowly status known as "box office poison". The likes of Meryl Streep, Michelle Pfeiffer and Glenn Close were now competing for the much-coveted role.

It was Christmas time in 1994 when it was announced that *Evita* was finally "on", and that British director Alan Parker would be taking the helm. Parker was a good choice; he had a string of music-orientated movies behind him including, *Bugsy Malone, Fame, Pink Floyd: The Wall*, and *The Commitments*. Madonna wasted no time in getting in touch with him.

"I remember sitting down... and writing an impassioned letter to Alan Parker, listing the reasons why I was the only one who could portray Eva (Evita was the nickname bestowed upon her by the Argentinean people), explaining that only I could understand her passion and her pain." Madonna has said that she felt some kind of supernatural drive to play this role – almost as if she was a woman possessed by the spirit of Eva Peron. "I can honestly say that I did not write this letter of my own free will. It was as if some other force drove my hand across the page."

Madonna had become obsessed with Eva because she recognised her as a kindred spirit. Both women had become synonymous with fame, power and controversy. "What drew me to the role from the beginning was the story of this remarkable woman, where she came from, how she came up in the world, the incredible amount of influence she had over an entire country and the impact she had on the world... I felt I could understand her."

The extraordinary parallels between the lives of Madonna and Eva are endless. Both came from humble, one-parent family origins; Eva was a poor farm girl who escaped to the big city of Buenos Aires when she was 15 years of age – to become an actress. Madonna arrived in the Big Apple when she was 17 – to become a dancer. Both managed to forge a series of amorous relationships that helped to propel them towards their goals. And both learned how to manipulate the media with spectacular results – inspiring a mixture of love and loathing.

Once Eva had married rising politician Juan Peron and helped him to secure his Presidential victory, she used her position to speak up for the rights of the poor – while Madonna used her celebrity to make a pitch for feminist and gay rights.

Alan Parker was understandably worried that "the level of Madonna's celebrity would get in the way of people seeing her as an actress playing a role." But after "several nerve-racking meetings" with the director, during which Madonna vowed she would sing, dance and act her heart out, she was told that the part was hers.

But Madonna knew that she had not been Andrew Lloyd Webber's first choice. "I don't think he was particularly thrilled with my singing abilities. I knew I was going in with odds against me. That's an awkward position to be in. You feel everyone's waiting for you to stumble."

And so it was make or break time for Madonna's acting career. And while Lloyd Webber considered the casting of Madonna to be something of a gamble – the movie itself was a gamble for all concerned. Movie musicals had become a dying art form; the last successful musical to come out of Hollywood had been *Grease* – way back in 1978. Would a modern-day audience have the patience to sit through an epic musical drama with no spoken dialogue?

Singing lessons were an obvious priority for

"Making Evita *was a real education, something on a different plane. I've never been so drained by anything. From the beginning I walked into another world – and kissed the world as I knew it goodbye."*

Madonna with Andrew Lloyd Webber and Tim Rice - the songwriting partnership behind *Evita*.

Facing page:
Madonna as Evita.

Madonna, as some of the musical's show-stopping songs were in a higher register than she was used to reaching. In the early half of 1995, Madonna brushed aside any plans that she had for a tour to promote her current 'Bedtime Stories' album, and instead spent six months improving her voice under the tutelage of world-famous voice coach Joan Lader. There was so much work to be done before the spirit of Peron could begin to express itself through Madonna. "I had to learn the score, train my voice, and master the tango before flying to London to record the soundtrack... I had butterflies in my stomach and I knew I was in for the ride of my life."

In October 1995, Madonna flew to London to record the film's soundtrack with her leading men: Antonio Banderas as Che, and Jonathan Pryce as Juan Peron. This was something of a humbling experience for Madonna, because she had no control over the process. "I'm used to writing my own songs, choosing the musicians, and saying what sounds good or doesn't. To work on all those songs... and not have a say was a big adjustment."

Each scene had to be rehearsed in England before the soundtrack could be recorded, so that the cast could grasp the kind of emotions that they needed to evoke in the songs. Sometimes Madonna would light candles and dim the studio lights in order to try and create an ethereal atmosphere. Months later, the cast would lip-synch the songs while shooting the scenes; a process that came naturally to Madonna, because of her experience with videos.

In January 1996 Madonna flew to Buenos Aires to "explore the myth of Eva Peron". She had hooked up with an Argentinean journalist in London who had agreed to arrange interviews with some of the people who had either known or worked with Eva – from childhood friends to work colleagues – as well as some anti-Peronists. Madonna took her research seriously; taking notes and videotaping conversations. She also recorded some of her experiences in a diary, which was later printed in *Vanity Fair* magazine.

In her entry for Saturday, January 13th she wrote: "Most (of the people who knew Eva Peron) are very old and I'm sure a good number will be quite suspicious of me. I can hardly blame them if the 'me' they know is the one they've read about in the newspapers. I am prepared to disarm all and get them to share their deepest, darkest secrets about Eva."

Madonna did indeed receive a hostile welcome. A wary government and a suspicious people had decided to close ranks against the whole *Evita* project, and as Madonna's car pulled away from the airport in Buenos Aires, she noticed that several walls has been daubed with graffiti messages that, roughly translated, said EVITA LIVES, GET OUT, MADONNA! "How's that for a welcome?" she recorded in her diary. "I have also read in the local newspapers that Alan Parker, Antonio Banderas and myself have been declared personae

non grata, which is a nice way of saying we are dirty rotten scum... None of this discourages me."

Devotees of Evita regarded the casting of Madonna as an outrage; for she still carried the baggage of her *Sex* book around with her. Casting a pop tart to play Santa Evita was sacrilege! It was also feared that the musical itself would further dishonour Evita's memory, because the storyline implied that she had slept her way to the top. Lloyd Webber and Rice had chosen to back the aristocracy's opinion of Eva when she married the President – that she was little more than opportunistic whore.

As Madonna began to try and unravel the tangled threads of Eva's life, she came to the conclusion that the musical was indeed a simplistic and unfair representation – and one that she didn't agree with. "I thought it was a male chauvinist point of view – that any woman who's powerful is a whore or slept her way to the top. There's that implication right through the musical and it's ludicrous."

Madonna has always argued that most men are terrified of powerful women, and can only cope with them by discrediting them. "It's the most obvious and predictable way out, to call a woman a whore and imply that she has no morals and no integrity and no talent. And God knows, I can relate to that."

The people that had known Eva Peron began to flesh out a much more fragile creature than Madonna had ever imagined; someone who had to carry around a lot of sadness and pain. "They humanised her for me. If you read the lyrics, she seems like a very one-dimensional, ambitious, power-hungry woman – without anything soft or vulnerable."

Eva Peron died from cancer in 1952 when she was only 33, sending the whole country into mourning. "I had nothing but compassion for Evita," concluded Madonna, "when I finally understood the poverty she came from, what she had to endure, and her illness... she suffered an enormous amount of pain while still working 18 hours a day. Her courage and strength of purpose were amazing." Repeatedly, people who had known Eva Peron kept telling Madonna how much she looked, and even moved, like her. Madonna merely had to wear brown contact lenses, a mouthpiece that disguised the gap between her front teeth, and a variety of wigs, in order to look the part. The *Evita* "look" encompassed pretty peasant dresses; functional Utility suits with shoulder pads, nipped in waists and knee-length skirts; and the extravagant evening dresses that were so much a part of Christian Dior's opulent "New Look", launched on the Paris catwalks in 1947.

And so Madonna became an ambassador for Eva – she was determined to convince Alan Parker of her findings, and to play the role in a sympathetic manner that would once again imbue Eva with some humanity and credibility. Because the current President of Argentina, Carlos Menem, had denounced the film and barred the crew from

Eva Peron, Argentine heroine.

shooting in certain key locations, Madonna embarked upon a diplomatic mission to woo the President. Somehow, she had to convince him of her sincere motivations.

Eventually, after several rebuffs, Madonna was granted a secret audience with the President. She was smuggled from her hotel, huddled onto the floor of a small car, driven to the airport and flown by helicopter to an island off the coast, where a clandestine champagne dinner had been arranged. Speaking through an interpreter, Madonna managed to turn the whole situation around. "I played him the soundtrack and immediately launched into this spiel about how passionate I was to make this movie, how fair I wanted to be, and how respectful I would be to Eva's memory."

After hours of conversation, during which President Menem maintained a relentless and seductive eye contact with Madonna, he held her face in his hands, kissed her on the cheeks and wished her good luck. "I was floating inside of the cabin the whole way home. He had worked his magic on me. I can only hope I did the same."

Madonna's mission opened up the way for negotiations, and the film crew were finally granted access to government buildings that were so crucial to the telling of the story, specifically the Casa Rosada, the presidential residence with the balcony from which Eva addressed her people. "I wanted to stand on that balcony with 5,000 people in that square and feel that feeling," said Madonna. "I knew that Eva had stood there, and that was so important – to stand where she stood."

Though she didn't know it then, the trials and obstacles that Madonna had endured so far were nothing compared to the dramas that were about to unfold during the making of *Evita*. Looking back, Madonna has acknowledged that the film was the most demanding experience in her entire career. "*Evita* was really a challenging, emotionally exhausting, and soul-searching couple of years for me."

To start with, her stay in Buenos Aires turned into a claustrophobic nightmare; lack of security when she first arrived resulted in Madonna being mobbed by fans and knocked to the ground. And because so many curious people hung around outside her hotel room each night, imploring her to make an Eva-style appearance on her balcony, she ended up having to move out of her suite – into a tiny room at the top of the building in order to get some sleep. If she ventured outside for a walk, people stared so intently at Madonna, that she felt too uncomfortable to continue. What's more, she had become a constant target of vicious journalism, and even received death threats from some extremists.

The city was wearing Madonna down. Surrounded by noise, cameras, bodyguards and police, her life had become as surreal a circus as the life of Eva Peron. Madonna's insomnia grew steadily worse, and the sweltering Argentine heat was a constant drain. In a telling diary entry, published in *Vanity Fair*, she wrote: "There are no words to describe the weariness I feel today. I have not slept well in days, and when I do, there is no comfort. My dreams are violent and full of betrayal. Like my life, there is no escape. I feel the weight of the responsibility of this film. I cannot talk about Evita and her life without defending myself... Dear God, what have I gotten myself into? What is happening to me?"

It seemed as if the soul connection between Madonna and Eva grew stronger as the film progressed. Madonna claimed that she could truly feel Eva's presence when she finally walked onto the balcony of the Casa Rosada to sing 'Don't Cry For Me Argentina' in front of thousands of people. "At that moment I felt her enter my body like a heat missile, starting with my feet, travelling up my spine, and flying out my fingertips, into the air, out to the people, and back up to heaven. Afterwards I could not speak and I was so happy. But I felt a great sadness too. Because she is haunting me. She is pushing me to feel things."

As the *Evita* bandwagon prepared to move location from steamy Buenos Aires to chilly Budapest – a fatigued and stressed Madonna stopped off to see her doctor in New York – and discovered something that was to turn her whole world upside down. She was 11 weeks pregnant, by her personal trainer Carlos Leon. And the timing could not have been worse.

Surprisingly for such a control freak, Madonna had become pregnant by mistake. Although she had wanted to have a child for years, she and Carlos had not (consciously) been "trying". Madonna experienced disbelief, elation and panic – in roughly that order. "It's just one of those weird surprises. I was so engrossed in making the movie that I wasn't paying attention to my body... any feelings of fatigue or strangeness I attributed to working too hard. I was tired and I'd sometimes feel a bit nauseous, but we were shooting outside and it was 100 degrees every day, and everyone was feeling a bit sick... I never, ever thought that I was pregnant."

Madonna confided in Alan Parker about her condition and they decided to keep the news quiet for as long as possible. If the press got hold of the story, a plague of journalists would storm Budapest and interfere with filming, and Madonna so wanted the project to continue in peace. She even kept the news from friends and family. But some of the crew would have to be told – some changes would have to be made to the shooting schedule – as well as to Madonna's wardrobe. Madonna wrote in her diary: "I must face the facts and tell Production because my costumes are starting not to fit, and I'm becoming very self-conscious about my body. Not to mention the fact that there are at least six more weeks of shooting and some big dance scenes to be filmed in England at the end of the schedule."

On Wednesday April 17, news of Madonna's condition leaked and her pregnancy became front-

Madonna during the filming of *Evita*.

Madonna with Carlos Leon, her personal trainer and father of her daughter Lourdes.

page news around the world. Madonna found this all rather tasteless. "I feel like my insides have been ripped open," she commented angrily. "The front page of the *Post*, CNN, even Hungarian radio. What's the big deal? Don't millions of women get pregnant every day?"

Filming in Budapest was not without its problems. The weather was freezing, and Madonna's legs ached constantly because she had to spend so many hours on her feet. And the bishop of a beautiful church had refused filming permission because (surprise) he did not approve of Madonna. By now, Madonna was in no mood for any diplomatic dealings. "I'm not grovelling for one more person in the name of this movie. There is no more skin left on my knees."

At the end of April, the film crew looked forward to enjoying the relative sanity and civility of their final location – London. Arrangements had been made for Madonna to stay in a large rented house in Holland Park, where she hoped to get a little peace and quiet. But it turned out that the house next door was in the process of being renovated – and the builders began banging and crashing around every morning at the fairly inhuman hour of 7.30. And as soon as Madonna's fans found out where she was staying, they started "making all sorts of irritating noises" outside.

Madonna's pregnancy was beginning to make her feel tired and uncomfortable at a time when she had some of her most demanding scenes to shoot. A big dance sequence caused dizzy spells and much anxiety. "There was a lot of jumping and sometimes I fell and I'd think 'I've done it this time', and I'd rush to the doctor to make sure everything was okay... It made me very protective of myself, and I think that helped my character, because Eva always had a lot of health problems... I could easily imagine being more frail."

Madonna was not only exhausted – her nerves were shot. She wasn't sure how much longer she could cope with being Eva. "Dare I say it? I am tired of being her."

Madonna had even developed a nervous stomach condition that was so debilitating that she sometimes had to lie down and recover in the middle of her scenes. She blamed the fervent nature of the film for the wear and tear on her body, mind and spirit. "The intensity of the scenes we've been shooting and the amount of emotional work and concentration that is needed to get through the day are so mentally and physically exhausting that I'm sure I will need to be institutionalised when it's over. I understand now why most actors are alcoholics, drug addicts, or Scientologists."

As the end of shooting was in sight, the cast and crew ran out of steam. "We're crawling through the last days," commented Madonna. "Alan walks around looking shattered." On Tuesday May 28 when Alan Parker announced the end of *Evita* by yelling "It's a wrap!", Madonna felt... nothing. She didn't feel the relief of such a monumental feat coming to end, or the ecstasy of a job well done, or the desire to celebrate. She just felt numb. "I wanted it all to end in a big crescendo. I wanted to hear trumpets and angels heralding my bravery. I wanted cast and crew members to flock to me imploring me to stay in touch. I wanted to throw myself on the ground and drown in my tears. But I was just too damn tired. And so was everyone else."

Madonna was back in America on Wednesday. For her final diary entry she wrote: "Have I solved the riddle of Evita? Why did she evoke such a strong response in people, then and now? Was she good or bad? Innocent or manipulative? I'm still not sure, But I know one thing – I have grown to love her."

Madonna and Eva had been good for each other. With her sympathetic handling of the role, Madonna had managed to restore some dignity to Lloyd Webber and Rice's tarnished vision of the icon. And, in return, Eva had managed to breathe new life into Madonna's flagging film career. Suddenly she was being hailed as the most potent female musical lead since Barbra Streisand. Not since the days of *Desperately Seeking Susan* had Madonna been so popular on screen.

Anyone who had ever doubted her ability as an actress only had to watch her heart-stopping performance as Eva on her death-bed, sobbing out her final lyrics in such a convincingly poignant scene. Not surprisingly, Madonna found herself being nominated for a Golden Globe award, and there were rumours that she might even be nominated for an Oscar. "I never doubted she could do it," praised Alan Parker, "But even I'm surprised at how well she's pulled it off."

After four years of floundering around in a kind of aprés-*Sex* wilderness, the tide of public opinion had finally turned back in favour of Madonna. People were now willing to forgive and forget that whole sordid business with Dita Parlo – the seedy alter ego with the gold tooth and the whip. If Dita had been the downfall of Madonna – then *Evita* was her salvation.

And then there was the pregnancy. Naturally, there were some journalists who accused Madonna of getting pregnant purely as a career move. Everyone wanted to know about her relationship with 29-year-old Cuban fitness trainer – Carlos Leon – whom she met while jogging in Central Park a few years back. Was Carlos merely a humble sperm donor who had agreed to sign away any paternal rights to the child (toy-boy stud mates with boy-toy superstar for a sure-fire beautiful baby), or was this a genuine love match with marriage in the air? Most journalists leaned towards the sperm donor theory.

Madonna shrugged off all this callous conjecture by saying, "It's all just part of the view the media likes to have of me. That I'm not a human being. That I don't have any feelings and don't really care for people. That I'm just ambitious, cold and calculating... I'm not surprised by it."

But Madonna was playing her cards close to her chest when it came to Carlos Leon; she refused to

Madonna triumphant - scenes from *Evita*.

"*Although 'Evita: The Complete Motion Picture Music Soundtrack' is not officially a new Madonna album, its success hinges on the singer's performance in the title role... Madonna's vocal abilities had never been the focus of her bumpy but never boring rise from New York discos to pop stardom, but the soundtrack puts the focus squarely on the leading lady's pipes. Andrew Lloyd Webber's compositions require a certain operatic flair and range that had not been required of Madonna before in her recording career... one comes away with a new admiration for her vocal skills.*"
Chicago Tribune, October 1996.

define the nature of their relationship. While she acknowledged that she thought Carlos was going to make a great father – she made none of the passionate declarations of love that were so forthcoming when she was about to marry Sean Penn. When Alan Jackson interviewed Madonna for *The Times* in October, he made this telling observation: "I waited in vain for even the smallest expression of love for Leon – if nothing verbal, then at least the merest hint of a smile at the mention of his name – or of an impulse towards coupledom. Nothing. And this nothingness – which contrasted with the ocean of tenderness for that extension of herself growing within makes me wonder if now she is just not too strong, too self-sufficient to allow a man to really share her life."

When questioned about her views on marriage, Madonna simply replied, "I don't know if I believe in it any more. I don't know what function it could have in my life."

Inevitably, the press began to sharpen its claws and sink its teeth into the "single mother" status of Madonna. They blamed her for being a bad influence on young girls; cited her as anti-family symbol; and accused her of contributing towards the destruction of the nuclear family. "People are extremely judgmental of me and my choice to have a child and not be married, as if I were the first person to do it. I know lots of married people who have terribly unhealthy relationships – I don't think marriage is a guarantee that your child is going to be happy."

For a woman so obviously obsessed with being in perfect shape, it was going to be an alarming experience for Madonna to watch her firm, flat "dream" stomach blow out like a balloon, and to feel encumbered by size and weight. Would she be able to grin and bear the bulge? Madonna has said that she veered from feeling like a million bucks one day – to feeling like a big fat pig the next. It was no longer possible to jog and lift weights – her fitness regime now had to focus on gentler forms of exercise – mainly walking, stretching and swimming. "It's difficult when you're used to being really fit and agile, having an enormous amount of energy and strength, and a really flat stomach. It's difficult when suddenly you have to surrender your body, and it's been a good lesson for me. It's given me license to relax in a way that I never really allowed myself to."

All Madonna could think about now was her baby. Motherhood was going to be both a learning and healing experience. "I didn't grow up with a mother and I envision hugging and tactile pleasure and the happiness of that. And I think how amazing to have someone in my life who's a part of me in a way that no one else can be."

On October 14, Madonna gave birth to a baby girl at the Good Samaritan hospital in Los Angeles. Because the paparazzi had staked out every maternity ward in the area, Madonna had to give the Press the slip by getting her publicist, Liz Rosenberg, to lead a decoy caravan of cars to another hospital in Santa Monica. Meanwhile, Madonna made a dash for the Good Samaritan and checked in under a bogus name. Already there was a price on her baby's head; $350,000 was the going rate for a first snapshot of Madonna's child.

Madonna had hoped to have a natural birth, but a caesarean had to be performed after 12 hours of painful labour. The baby was named Lourdes Maria Ciccone Leon (Lola for short) after the French village where the Virgin Mary is said to have appeared to St. Bernadette and, incidentally, after one of the fantasy characters in Madonna's *Sex* book. "Lourdes was a place that my mother had a connection to. People were always sending her holy water from there. She always wanted to go there but never did."

The premiere for *Evita* took place in Los Angeles on December 14 at the Shrine Auditorium. Madonna arrived wearing a glamorous rose-coloured Evita-style dress, designed by Givenchy, and declared that she felt like Cinderella. An enthusiastic and star-studded audience applauded the songs and performances, and when the film went on release across America, it took a grand total of $8.6 million over the first weekend, enough to finish in second place on the box-office report.

The New Year could not have got off to a better start for Madonna; she was awarded a Golden Globe for Best Actress in a Musical or Comedy – but Hollywood chose to climb aboard its high horse and snub her when it came to the mighty Oscars. Unbelievably, Madonna didn't even receive a nomination. But she was asked to make an appearance, singing the Oscar nominated song "You Must Love Me". Madonna gave the performance of her lifetime on that night. In spite of the deep disappointment that she must have been feeling for being passed over – Madonna managed to steal the show with her emotional rendering of the song – and a dignity and strength of spirit that defied the Hollywood elite.

In May 1997 – just seven months after the birth of their baby – Madonna and Carlos split up. While Carlos would always play a paternal role in the life of Lourdes, he was no longer Madonna's official live-in lover.

They were said to have drifted apart. "You meet people, you fall in love with them, you decide to have a child, but you can't predict the future," she said resignedly. "It's sad, it's not an ideal situation... but Carlos is still very much a part of Lourdes' life, so I don't feel she's being deprived of anything."

After all that she had been through recently, it was time to take a break. For once in her life, Madonna had no plans. She wanted to spend less time working and more time getting to know her daughter. "The most important thing right now is her, not me. That fact trivialises all the other silly little things that used to bother me, like the nasty things people say about me in the newspapers. It's like a built-in bliss factor. You can just go, 'So what?' Which is great. It regulates everything."

'Best Actress in a Musical or Comedy' at the Golden Globe Awards, January 1997.

Facing page: **Madonna and** *Evita* **co-star Antonio Banderas.**

This is a
ticket
for two
to see
'HAIR'
DISCOTHEQUE

German silent movie actress Dita Parlo… a major influence on the *Sex* scandal.

Rossetti's 'Proserpine' of 1874. Cascades of hair were a common characteristic of Pre-Raphaelite paintings… and Madonna in 1998.

Madonna shocked her public in the early Nineties by drawing on bondage and lesbian imagery for her *Sex* book. Had she gone too far this time?

Madonna's *Ray Of Light* album saw the former Material Girl look to the East and developing an interest in all things spiritual. The world's most famous Catholic pop star has now also embraced Buddhism.

Below: Lourdes, site of the miraculous appearance of the Virgin Mary to St. Bernadette, and inspiration for the name of Madonna's baby.

Below: Traditional Hindu paintings of Krishna influenced Madonna's 'Indian Summer' photoshoot for *Rolling Stone* in July 1998 *(above left)*.

INFLUENCES & HEROES/PART 5

EARTH MOTHER

There comes a time in most people's lives when they are pricked by a metaphysical urge to start asking those big and meaningful questions about life. Who am I? Why am I here? What's it all for? As Madonna took time out to raise her daughter and found herself approaching that daunting "landmark" age of 40, she entered a mid-life "meaning of life" crisis and, much to everyone's surprise, the Material Girl emerged from all this soul-searching a mature and Ethereal Girl. "The whole idea of giving birth and being responsible for another life put me in a different place, a place I'd never been before."

Since the making of Evita and the birth of her daughter, Madonna had chosen to step back from her life as a celebrity, and keep busy behind the scenes running her Maverick empire, a multi-media company formed in 1992 that, after a slow start, now boasted an impressive roster of acts including Alanis Morissette and Prodigy. And then, in 1998, Madonna staged a spectacular comeback with a new studio album called *Ray Of Light* – her first since 1994's *Bedtime Stories*.

Not only did Madonna unveil a completely new image for this comeback – she had a new personality to match. The latest surge of interviews revealed her to be a much calmer, and less combative character than she had ever been before; bursting to discuss the joys of motherhood and her passion for all things spiritual. This "New Age" Madonna seemed keen to step down from her pedestal and admit that she was a mere mortal after all – someone vulnerable and perhaps even approachable. An embarrassment of fame and riches had failed to make her as

happy as she'd always hoped; something intangible was missing, and so she had started to "turn inwards" on a journey of self discovery.

In the past, Madonna had always been far too 'antsy' and impetuous to sit still for even a second and try to tune into herself. But the birth of her daughter had forced her to slip her life into a calmer gear; the demands of breast feeding had to take priority over Madonna's work schedule. "I would say the beginning of my search and my spiritual journey... really kicked into first gear with the impending birth of my daughter and coming to a realisation that I really didn't think I knew that much at all. And I felt like I had so much to learn... I started studying the Kabbalah (a Jewish mystical teaching), and I started practising yoga, and I started kind of reading lots of different literature. It all sort of happened at once, and I don't think that there are any accidents. I think it happened to me for a reason. Like the teachers arrived because the student was ready to listen." Madonna was an Earth Mother. She had tapped into the newly dawned Age of Aquarius and become pop's Shirley Maclaine, forever dropping words like "raised consciousness" and "karma" into conversations.

The video for her new single 'Frozen', shot in the Mojave Desert and inspired by scenes from the film *The English Patient*, presented one of Madonna's most exciting (and accessible) new images for years. She looked like a high priestess of the New Hippie movement in her dark and mysterious cloak; her hands and feet decorated with elaborate ethnic patterns, (dyed with henna using an Indian form of body painting called Mehndi). Her hair was now

"People have been obsessed with the idea that I'm reinventing myself; I'd rather think that I'm slowly revealing myself, my true nature. It feels to me like I'm just getting closer to the core of who I really am."

Facing page: **A heavily pregnant Madonna out walking, 1996.**

Following pages: **Madonna at the Golden Globe Awards, Los Angeles, January 1998.**

Princess Diana, whose hounding by the press struck a chord with Madonna, inspiring her 'Drowned World' video.

long, wavy and flowing; shades of orange blending with shades of strawberry blond. Madonna could have stepped straight out of a Pre-Raphaelite painting by Gabriel Rossetti. (And if you looked very closely, the famous beauty spot above Madonna's upper lip had mysteriously disappeared!) Though 'Frozen' sounded like a simple love song, it could be taken on a much deeper level. "It really says that you can't attract good things and happiness if you don't have an open heart; if we're consumed by material things – if we feel envy and jealousy – we can't reach happiness."

This latest Madonna incarnation was something of a shock to most people, especially when confronted with the woman in the flesh. When a journalist called Sylvia Patterson from *NME* interviewed Madonna and found her wrapped in an ethnic blanket with Sanskrit squiggles for the word "Om" painted all over her hands, she described her thus: "The hair is unwashed and black-rooted, an oily centre-parting pulled severely into two milk maid's pleats tied at the end with elastic bands. She is wearing no make-up. Her eyebrows are thin, as are the lips. This is Madonna, most fabulous female superstar in the history of popular music, in 1998. And she looks like a casualty newly staggered down from the Glastonbury healing fields at 7am after a three-day acid trip bender... she cannot be a hippie, not Madonna, not Pop's Big Sister, not she who is Pop Culture itself... imposter!"

Lyrically, Madonna was in a contemplative, navel gazing kind of mood for *Ray of Light*, reviewing her life, her disappointments and her search for love with a refreshingly open-hearted sincerity. Of all her albums, *Ray of Light* became the one that people wanted to sit down and digest; picking over the lyrics and analysing their deeply personal meanings. "I'm trying to affect people in a quieter way. I set out to be honest about where I am now. I was only trying to deal with my truth right now."

Spin magazine declared Madonna's new album to be her "most radical, mask-free work", and *Rolling Stone* agreed that this was her best album in years. Co-produced and mostly co-written by Orbital's William Orbit, the spacey trip-hop sounds were the perfect accompaniment to Madonna's cosmic stream of consciousness. "The last two years have been like a ray of light to me... I feel like I'm starting my life over in some ways. My daughter's birth was like a rebirth for me."

The opening track 'Drowned World'/'Substitute For Love' is a startlingly frank appraisal of the pros and cons of fame – the high price one pays for being rich and famous – the crosses that an icon has to bear. This song is Madonna's attempt to come to terms with her fame, and to understand its place in her life. "I traded fame for love/Without a second thought/It all became a silly game/Some things cannot be bought/Got exactly what I wanted/Wanted it so badly/Running, rushing back for more/I suffered fools/So gladly/And now I found/I've changed my mind."

Madonna admitted that while she had been blessed with so much, and wouldn't trade her life for anything, certain fundamental things were missing. "A lot of people have a false impression that if you're famous somehow you're going to feel this incredible sense of fulfilment. That you're going to be truly loved and truly happy... But anyone who is famous could probably tell you that the opposite is true. If you aren't really truly fulfilled, and you don't have intimacy in your life, and you don't know how to love, then thousands of people adoring you actually makes you feel emptier. Fame can become a substitute for love for a lot of people... but in the end, that's not what it is at all."

In an interview for *Esquire* magazine, Madonna once talked about the loneliness that performers feel when they come off stage, having soaked up the adoration of a huge crowd, and then finding themselves trapped inside a hotel. "You go up to your room, and you can't go out because you're too famous to go out without everyone following you and 20 bodyguards, so you sit in your room while everyone else has fun being anonymous... and you feel the most unbelievable loneliness. Yes, everyone adores you in a kind of mass-energy way, but then you're absolutely separated from humanity. It's the most bizarre irony."

Yes, money made it possible for Madonna to stay in the finest suites in the grandest hotels and to live in palatial surroundings – but she still couldn't step out on the street without being followed everywhere by obsessive fans and pushy photographers – without being stared at by curious onlookers. She was the proverbial princess trapped in an ivory tower. "At times I wish I could be more spontaneous and just go outside my gate. But I try to make a point of saying dammit, I'm going to do it anyway. I don't care if there's 60 people outside my apartment in New York; I'm going out for a walk, and if they follow me, they follow me. I will not be a prisoner."

Madonna used to cite Princess Diana as the only other woman in the world who could possibly understand what it felt like to be caged in this way; to be hounded incessantly by the paparazzi. The two women met once at a charity cocktail party in London at the time when Madonna was recording the soundtrack for *Evita*. "We must have talked for about ten minutes. I said I had always sympathised with her position, and made some joke about how the only person who seemed to get more attention than me was her. She said, 'I think you handle the press better than I do,' and I said 'You will have to get skin as thick as an armadillo.' She said: 'We must get together and you can tell me how.'"

But they never did meet again. And when Madonna heard about Diana's death she told *The Times*, "I have been chased through that same tunnel so many times that I have lost count... anyone who has ever been chased like that, and who has had to live that sort of life hit the wall with her."

Madonna's video for 'Drowned World'/'Substitute For Love' was a powerful attempt to communicate the horror of celebrity; the haunted, hunted feeling of being constantly surrounded by staring eyes and the invasive glare of flashbulbs popping in your face. The parallels with Princess Diana are shockingly and movingly obvious. In the video, Madonna sits dejectedly in the back of a chauffeur-driven car, hiding behind her long hair and a pair of dark sunglasses, while photographers pursue her on motorbikes. Everywhere she goes she is stared at – and it's interesting to note that she chooses to portray the faces of these onlookers as vile, disfigured freaks. When Madonna finally reaches the sanctuary of her private apartment, relief sweeps across her face as she reaches out and cuddles a little girl with long dark hair that is supposed to be Lourdes.

Madonna has said that Lourdes has been an incredible healing influence on her life. When she was once asked if she worried about how she was going to protect her daughter, Madonna replied, "It's the other way around. She protects me." Several songs on the new album were inspired by Lourdes. 'Nothing Really Matters' is a song about Madonna's realisation that the most important thing in life is loving people and sharing love, and 'Little Star' is a joyous expression of her new-found happiness with her daughter. "Now I really want to stay alive forever, I mean, she comes first. That's how it's changed my perspective – and everything else falls behind it. It's changed my priorities, and I'm sure it will affect every decision I make until I die."

For obvious reasons, Madonna has guarded her daughter's privacy fiercely, trying to bring her up in as "normal" a way as possible by keeping her out of the spotlight. From the very beginning, Madonna made it quite clear that her daughter was not for public consumption. "They (the media) are not going to have access to her in the way that they have to me." But that hasn't meant that Lourdes has had to be excluded from Madonna's working life; she attends photo sessions, and she was there in the studio during the making of *Ray Of Light*. "I try to take her with me every time I travel. She's starting to speak and as she's always surrounded by Hispanics and Italians, she doesn't speak a word of English yet. But she knows tons of Spanish. Don't forget that her dad is Cuban, that I live in Miami, and most of my friends are Hispanic."

Madonna and child are forced to live mostly in her new Los Angeles home in Los Feliz. "It's the dullest town, therefore there isn't much going on, therefore there aren't a lot of paparazzi hanging about. It's the one place I totally get left alone." Madonna has another home in Coconut Grove in Miami, and it was here that she finally agreed to let herself be photographed with Lourdes in a series of exclusive first portraits for the March issue of *Vanity Fair*. The magazine described Madonna as "a woman on the verge of becoming herself" and featured a beautiful picture of her sitting with Lourdes on her lap; a dark-eyed child with olive skin, an inquisitive smile and a mop of curly hair.

When *Vanity Fair* asked if she would like to have another child, she said, "Yes, but I'd like to be in a stable relationship. Sometimes you want to look over at somebody and say, 'What do you think we should do?'" And on the subject of Lourdes' father, Carlos Leon, Madonna confirmed that he was still a constant presence in her daughter's life. "We are friends. And I'm very happy. It took a while for us to get to this place."

Madonna believes that it will take a courageous man indeed to commit himself to a relationship with her; for while there seemed to be no shortage of lovers who wanted to experience the temporary thrill of basking in her spotlight – finding someone with staying power was another matter. "People probably look at me and think, 'Oh God, she can have whatever she wants. She lives in a really fast-paced way. She's probably independent. She doesn't need anyone.' It adds up to a pretty frightening place for most people to want to step into."

Madonna's new substitute for love had become her spiritual quest, and she was eager to share her metaphysical findings in her songs. "I don't want to sound egotistical or anything like that... but I do think that if I've been enlightened, and I truly feel like I've been enlightened, then it's my responsibility to share what I know with other people."

Three songs on *Ray Of Light* ('Drowned World', 'Swim' and 'Mer Girl') are concerned with the healing element of water; the album cover is drenched in ocean blue and Madonna wears a shiny wet-look dress. "There's water in birth and there's water in baptism and when you go into the bath or the ocean there's a feeling of cleansing, a feeling of starting all over again. Being new, being healed. That's sort of what's going on in my life and I'm exploring that element in my songwriting."

Madonna's exercise regime had also undergone a spiritual transformation. She had swapped her gruelling gym routine for the tortuous "lotus" position and become a devotee of yoga; the ancient Indian discipline that stretches body, mind and spirit. "When I gave birth to my daughter, I had a caesarean, and I couldn't go back to working out the way I used to. A friend turned me on to yoga... when I first started I couldn't do any of the poses. I used to call the balancing positions 'the humiliation positions.' I just kept falling and falling. Then little by little I got there... Yoga teaches me how to be humble and patient. It makes me strong both inside and outside."

One of the songs on *Ray Of Light*, 'Shanti/Ashtangi', is inspired by the Sanskrit prayers that Madonna chants before her yoga sessions (though some Sanskrit experts jumped on her pronunciation.) "The idea is that even if you don't understand the words and you just learn them by hearing and memorising them, that the saying of the word, the vibration that occurs in your body from saying it, actually brings a feeling of bliss and happiness." In the July issue of *Rolling Stone*, Madonna appeared in a psychedelic portfolio of photographs, taken by David LaChapelle, that

Life in the media spotlight. Madonna steps out.

Each level gets further and further away from the material world, or the world of the senses, and goes more and more into the spiritual world. And so I feel like I'm just moving more in that area in terms of exploring. Which isn't to say that I'm not interested in sex!"

Madonna was keen to point out that she had not turned her back on Catholicism. Instead, she had come to the conclusion that all paths lead to God. "There are indisputable truths that connect all religions, and I find that very comforting. My spiritual journey is to be open to everything... I believe that God is in all of us and that we are all capable of being gods and goddesses. That's my brand of Catholic mysticism. Throw some Buddhism in there and you've got my religion."

Of course, there were those who accused Madonna of using spirituality as a very necessary career move. After the publication of her *Sex* book back in 1992, she had managed to alienate her audience by presenting them with a disturbing piece of work; insisting that it was full of positive messages, and then stubbornly refusing to see why people were so upset by it. But six years later, she had become a wiser and warmer creature, willing to admit that she sometimes made mistakes. Madonna had come full circle. "In the beginning of my career I just did whatever I wanted to and if it made me feel good, if it was fun, that was cool. Now I feel like everything we do... affects society in a potent way. I feel a sense of responsibility because my consciousness has been raised."

But Madonna views the whole *Sex* episode as a necessary chapter in her life. "I've been incredibly petulant, incredibly self-indulgent, incredibly naïve. But I needed to do all of those things to get where I am now, and where I am now I'm very happy with. I don't have any regrets, even though there are moments when I go, 'Oh, God, I can't believe I said that or did that.' But you know what? I have to love that person too. She brought me here."

In 1998, Madonna seemed happy to become a humble pop star again, and when one journalist asked her to describe her passion for music, she made it sound better than sex. "It's like an adrenaline rush, like a drug. When you're writing something and you know it's good, you get flushed, you can feel the blood coursing through your veins, you feel alive, all your nerve endings stand up, something just clicks... I think that's why people love music so insanely. It does, as they say, soothe the savage beast."

Once again, Madonna had become an inspiring role model for women. This post-feminist-New-Age guru-icon was learning how to keep her ego in check and see the bigger picture of life. Her new *Ray Of Light* album was both a huge critical and commercial success, and her fan mail had never been more positive. And as she turned 40, she had never looked better in her life. Anyone undergoing a mid-life crisis of their own only had to look at her to see that life really could begin at 40.

Mother and child: Madonna with daughter Lourdes, photographed in Paris, 1998.

Facing page: **Madonna the Ethereal Girl.**

Following page: **Opening the 1998 San Remo Festival with 'Frozen' from her new album** *Ray of Light.*

were obviously inspired by her love of yoga. Entitled "Madonna's Indian Summer", the pictures attempted to recreate the fantastic imagery that's found in the Hindu paintings of Lord Krishna, with Madonna dressed in vibrantly coloured saris, and twisting her arms, hands and fingers into impossibly graceful positions.

Madonna had become like a spiritual sponge, eager to soak up all the mystical wonders of world religions. She was especially interested in the wisdom found in the Jewish Kabbalah, and began to wear a red string round her left wrist in order to demonstrate her kinship for its principles of friendship, spirituality and knowledge. "In the Kabbalah there's Ten Sefirots, or ten levels of consciousness.